Puppy Love

Puppy Love

Frank Barham

Bridgeview Press
Philadelphia

Somewhere in the rain, there will always be an abandoned dog that prevents you from being happy.

Aldous Huxley

The greatness of a nation and its moral progress can be judged by the manner in which its animals are treated.

Mahatma Gandhi

TABLE OF CONTENTS

Introduction

The stories in *Puppy Love* are based on real animal encounters by the author over a period of four winters in the fishing village of Chuburna Puerto located on the northern shore of the Yucatan Peninsula of Mexico.

Chapter I

Chico

The image of the grim reaper is ubiquitous—a hooded human skeleton carrying a scythe in one hand as the other curls a bony finger in an invitation to approach death, but did you know death's image is species specific? That fateful morning of January, 2006, the grim reaper stalked the beach on four bony paws. For which dog had it come? Only time would tell.

Glistening above wet sea shells, wavy bands of heat rose from the beach causing the brilliant-blue Mexican sky to shimmer. Bowing to nature's morning schedule, the land breeze crept north across the Yucatecan scrub jungle in search of the sea. Palm branches barely moved in its slow wake as the heat of the day intensified. I sensed we were in for a hot and humid Monday—a day to remain in the shade— especially for vulnerable creatures large or small.

In the fishing village of Chuburna Puerto, situated on the northwestern shore of Mexico's Yucatan Peninsula, my construction project neared the halfway point.

On the way to the work site, I stopped at a local *tienda* and purchased a sandwich and a bottle of water. I also purchased a bag of dog treats, which I would later toss to starving feral dogs I would encounter along the road.

Strays were an everyday occurrence. I had great sympathy for these dogs, particularly the pregnant or nursing ones. Their bony rib cages and bloated bellies identified their state of chronic starvation. My heart ached for these mother-dogs whose minimal fat stores and scrawny muscles were being converted into milk to feed their puppies.

Local people drove these dogs away from their villages and often went out of their way to hide food scraps and keep water from stray animals. These feral dogs were destined to starve to death or succumb to diseases (secondary to poor nutrition). They often die a slow, pitiful death at an early age.

When a feral mother-dog dies, her helpless puppies are left to fend for themselves. Her death means there is no one to defend the pups from predators—primarily large birds. Without her milk or guidance to water, puppies can die of starvation or thirst in a matter of days.

I questioned myself about feeding stray dogs. Was I contributing to the number of feral animals? Maybe. Nevertheless, I could not ignore starving dogs that, in some cases, were being used up in order to make milk for their defenseless offspring. Sadly, in 2006, there were no animal rescue organizations in the Yucatan Peninsula to help feral mother-dogs or their pups.

I wandered alone around my construction site, assessing the work completed on the house the day before. Within minutes of my arrival, workmen arrived then began another day of creating art from the simplest of building materials. They hand mixed cement then moved it, via a bucket brigade, onto the roof where the grey slurry mixed with worker's sweat. They poured the thick liquid over a cement-block roof then left it to dry.

Loose sand, stirred by the flip-flop clad feet of Mexican laborers, swirled about in tornado-like eddies across the unpaved courtyard, making one wish for goggles. Dashing about, workers performed various tasks intermittently interrupted by periods of boisterous laughter. One man sang an off-key song about his alleged sexual escapades. A few of the workers joined in the chorus as others whistled the tune and wiped sweat.

The pace of work quickened around me. I felt I was in the way, so I retreated to the interior of the unfinished front building destined to become my living room, dining room and kitchen. There I found shade from the blazing sun. I peered out an opening in the wall that would soon be a window. I rested my elbows on the future windowsill and watched the laborers work their magic.

In a matter of a few hours, the temperature rose to ninety degrees Fahrenheit as the tolerable level of humidity rose to a hot stickiness. Without looking at my watch, I could tell the hour neared 12:00 p.m. because the land breeze had begun to subside. In an hour or so, the breeze would come from the ocean, but during the transition, there would be little or no breeze, which I referred to as natures air-conditioning.

In the midst of the noise, heat, and construction activity, I had an uncomfortable feeling of being watched. The feeling grew in intensity. I felt more and more ill at ease—downright uncomfortable. I shifted my weight, repositioned my elbows, and looked about. I saw nothing unusual. I scanned the top of the rear bedroom building, which stood across the courtyard. I saw no one. I scanned the beach behind me and saw no one.

With growing discomfort, I looked at the ground beneath the opening where I rested my elbows. There I discovered the cause of my discomfort. Some "thing" starred up at me. At first, I thought I saw a collection of red balloons—the kind twisted into animal shapes by a clown at a birthday party. I blinked once, twice, and a third time. My first impression morphed into reality.

Semi-erect and attempting to stand on wobbly and thin legs, I saw a puppy maybe eight weeks old. Despite the problems besieging the small, trembling creature, my gaze met a pair of sad, brown eyes. The puppy's eyelids were swollen and oozed yellow pus whose crusting helped seal the upper and lower lids to a narrow slit. I had difficulty trying to ascertain that the animal's eyes were brown. The puppy had the worst cases of pink-eye, or conjunctivitis, I had ever seen. Because of the swollen, crusted lids, the animal could barely see.

Its jowls drooped in despair. I had never seen such a sad countenance. For a second, my disbelief fell like an obscuring curtain. I had to force myself to look at the animal. Suddenly, I felt a terrible sense of doubt about what I should do. Pity swept over me causing my heart to ache.

My initial impression of a "red balloon dog" was based on the puppy's bloated abdomen and bright-red, hairless skin. Later, I would learn the reddened skin, called red mange, was caused by an infection similar to human scabies. The canine variety is caused by parasitic invasion of hair follicles causing a generalized inflammation of the skin resulting in reversible hair loss—if treated.

In addition to the redness of the puppy's in-flamed skin, there were numerous crusted sores that peppered the puppy's body. I could see a few areas of naturally brown or black skin now reddened by in-

16

flammation. The dog's body was meant to be covered with a spotted coat of black, brown, and white hair, but not a single hair remained.

Until that time, I had never seen a skin condition to equal that of this puppy. Whatever the condition's name, it had caused severe itching. There were numerous infected scratch marks all over the puppy's flanks—any place reachable by a scratching paw. Further observation revealed the puppy had no discernible muscles on his long, spindly legs, hip, or shoulder areas. They had wasted away, secondary to starvation, pre-and post-birth. The spiky bones of its spine threatened to pierce the taunt skin covering its back.

Head to tail, the puppy had multiple problems including the fact he had only a stub of a tail. Missing any evidence of a scar or recent amputation, I presumed he had been born without the usual anatomical finial.

No doubt, the puppy had been starving for some time and appeared to be dehydrated. He looked exhausted and struggled to stand. Nevertheless, he trudged forward, hugging the outside wall of the building where I sheltered from the sun. He too needed to escape the sun's heat. I could only imagine how the sun's searing heat felt on its inflamed skin. With each tenuous, troubled step, the puppy risked toppling over.

Across the hot sand, he trudged toward a stack of timbers leaning against the building. Once the puppy reached the safety of the lumber pile, with its dappled shade, he dropped onto the sand with an audible "ugh." I feared he had died.

I wondered how he had survived as long as he had. Rainfall in the Yucatan had been almost non-existent that winter. That meant there were no rain puddles from which animals could drink, and no villager would dare feed or provide water to such a puppy.

I wondered where he had come from or why he had wandered onto my property given all the commotion and noise associated with construction. He seemed unfazed by the clatter of construction and the clamor of workmen who scurried about either oblivious to his presence or unconcerned about his condition. Did the puppy equate human activity with food and water?

I went to my car and got my bag of dog treats and bottle of water. Severely dehydrated, he needed the water more than I did. Like him, the treats were dry. I hoped he had the energy to chew them.

I searched the area for something I could use as a water bowl but found nothing. I decided to borrow two of the worker's shovels, which I would use in lieu of bowls. Using sand as a scouring agent, I cleaned rust and bits of dried concrete from the spades. After ten minutes of scouring, the shovels shined like polished silver. I now had something I could use to feed and water the puppy.

Dog treats in hand, I crept toward the puppy. Illuminated by narrow shafts of sunlight, filtered through gaps between sheltering planks, the puppy's body almost disappeared in the shadows. As I approached it, he cowered, drawing himself into a ball. Is he afraid of me? I asked myself.

His reaction gave me the impression he had been physically abused, possibly beaten, or chased by local villagers, so I backed away a few feet. I crumbled the treats into puppy sized bites, placed them on a shovel, pushed it close to his nose, and then backed away. I didn't want to further frighten the shivering animal.

Mustering all his energy, the puppy extended its scrawny neck and shaking head toward the food. First, he sniffed the largest fragment then his tongue explored its texture before taking it into his mouth.

That has to be his first food in who knows how many days, I thought.

Laboriously, his thin, sharp teeth managed to crush the treats, which he swallowed with difficulty. As he struggled to ingest the dry food, a lump grew in my throat. I too swallowed hard, but I would have been hard pressed to describe my joy on seeing the puppy chew the food.

As I sat down on the sand, I called to one of the workers, "Would you please slide that cleaned shovel toward me, bowl side up?"

The worked slid the shovel my way. I poured a few ounces of bottled water into the faux water bowl and then slid the shovel toward the puppy.

He either sensed or smelled the water because he suddenly appeared alert. I pushed the shovel blade close to his nose. Barely moving his head, his tongue darted toward the liquid. He didn't have the strength to stand and drink, so I pushed the shovel closer and raised its handle skyward. This caused the water to flow toward the edge of the blade and the puppy's mouth.

Without raising his head, the puppy extended his pale pink tongue into the water then lapped it up. From his awkward prone position, his tiny tongue moved in slow, curling motions, carrying small amounts of water from shovel to mouth. After consuming about an ounce, he dropped his head, just short of the shovel's edge, and exhaled a long sigh. He lay still; his chest, motionless.

Oh my God, he's dead.

Suddenly, as though resurrected, the puppy took a breath. His bony chest rose and fell a fraction of an inch. Drinking and eating had exhausted him. Fatigue's sleep had overtaken him. I decided to let him sleep.

As the workday came to a close, workers prepared to leave for home. Hugo, the night watchman, arrived. He would sleep on site to make sure no one stole construction supplies—especially expensive concrete blocks or cement. His brutish appearance and strong build, resulting from his primary job of octopus fishing and part-time construction work, would frighten away most would be thieves.

I informed him about the puppy's presence and pointed out his resting place. "Do you know if there is a veterinarian nearby?" I asked.

"No," Hugo said, shaking his head. "You have to go into Merida for a vet."

Turning to the workmen, I asked, "Do any of you know of a nearby vet?"

The workers shook their heads.

I had no idea where I could get help or what to do for the hairless ball-of-suffering. I knew he needed help, but I didn't know where to find it. After all, medical attention for locals required them to travel many miles.

Just before departing, one worker said, "I think there's a vet in Progreso."

"Thanks," I said. "I'll inquire there."

"Hugo," I called, pointing toward the window sill where I had left the bag of treats. "When the pup wakes up, give him some water and bits of those dog treats. Make sure you look in on him before you go to sleep, and remember, stray dogs may be attracted to the water in the shovel. Make sure it's full and please listen for cries of distress during the night."

I was afraid a larger animal or a rat might see the defenseless pup as a meal.

"I'll keep an eye on him," Hugo said. "Don't worry. He'll be fine."

"I know you leave around seven in the morning,

but would you please make sure there's food and water for the pup before you leave? I won't be here until about mid-afternoon."

Hugo nodded. "Don't worry. I'll take good care of him. I'll make sure he has food and water."

Later that afternoon, I left the worksite feeling depressed and unsure of what I would be able do for the puppy. I needed time to formulate a plan. Since I didn't know what had caused the pup's skin condition, I didn't want to touch him. I was concerned his disease might be contagious. I also wondered if picking up the puppy, with some kind of cloth to protect my hands, would hurt or damage his inflamed skin. If I were to pick him up, what would the pressure do to his bloated abdomen? These unanswered concerns were due to my ignorance of the dog's diagnosis.

On the way to my hotel in Progresc, the main seaport in the Yucatan, I stopped at a restaurant owned by an English-speaking husband-wife team— Joe and Maryann. Both were rumored to have been college professors in Canada. They had immigrated to Mexico, three years earlier, in search of a slower, cheaper lifestyle. Everything about their dress, demeanor, and attitude screamed *gringo* turned Mexican.

Over dinner, I told the couple of the day's happenings.

"Joe," I said, "I need your help. Is there a local veterinarian who might help me with the puppy?"

Before Joe could answer, Maryann interrupted. "Beatrice should be able to help." Maryann waved toward the bar where Joe washed glasses. "Joe, get the phonebook."

"Huh," Joe said and walked from behind the bar to a corner table where he fumbled with some papers. Moments later he announced, "Here it is."

"Look up Puppy Palace's phone number,"

21

Maryann said, looking up from her cell phone. "I don't have her number on this thing."

Joe thumbed through the tattered and yellowed pages of a thin book.

Maryann yelled, "Hurry up! Frank doesn't have all night. Besides, his dinner is getting cold."

"That's okay, Maryann," I said, patting the air to indicate she shouldn't worry. "I have time."

Joe continued to thumb through the tattered phone book.

"Give me that!" Maryann snarled as her hand darted toward the book.

Joe's arm recoiled, saving the book from his wife's clutch.

"For Christ's sake, keep your knickers on, woman," he said. "I'm looking as fast as I can. If you wrote more legibly, I wouldn't have so much damn trouble reading this scribble."

"I knew his hearing was going," Maryann whispered and winked at me. "Now, I'm beginning to think his eyesight is failing too."

"I found it!" Joe said. "Here it is."

Maryann snatched the book from Joe's hand. "Let me see."

She handed me a scrap of paper and a pen. "Now write this down," she said. "Her number is 52-1-858-3652. I know she'll be happy to help. She has a soft spot for dogs—especially puppies."

"Thanks," I said pushing the folded paper in my shirt pocket. "It's late, so I'll call her in the morning."

I had difficulty going to sleep that night. I worried about the puppy.

I managed to fall asleep around 2:00 a.m.

I awoke at ten o'clock. After breakfast, I phoned the veterinarian. She spoke to me at great length about the puppy's condition. "The skin condition is

22

called red mange. It's common throughout the area, but it's not very contagious for humans. However, the pup's secondary skin infections could be serious for him and you."

"How should I handle him?" I asked.

"Don't let the dog's infected skin have contact with your skin if it is abraded or you have cuts. Use a towel or rubber gloves to pick up the puppy. Make sure they're cheap, since you'll throw them away after they've been used."

The vet agreed to see the puppy in her clinic that afternoon.

After a leisurely cup of coffee, I placed an ice chest in the trunk of my car then started my scheduled stops. Before I visited the building supply house, I purchased my usual luncheon sandwich, a large bottle of water, and a bag of dog treats. To my usual shopping list, I added a bag of ice, a pint of milk and two small bowls for the puppy's water and milk.

I also purchased two cheap towels and a pair of rubber gloves to use as rescue tools.

I arrived at the beach at 2:00 p.m. and hurried to the wood pile. I looked under it, expecting to find the puppy curled up and fast asleep. Much to my surprise, he wasn't there. My heart sank.

"Has anyone seen the puppy," I asked the men, working near the wood pile.

They said that they hadn't seen the puppy. Much to my chagrin, they appeared unconcerned. I wondered, doesn't anyone give a damn?

I couldn't believe the puppy had strayed far, so I asked several workmen to join me in a search. Two of the workmen went east and two went west along the beach. Several other men went south to search around nearby houses.

My instructions were, "Look under anything that

might provide protection and shade for a puppy. If you find him, don't approach him—just find me and tell me his location."

"How far do you want us to search?" Pedro asked, removing his ball cap to wipe his brow.

I thought for a moment. "Not more than three blocks if you have time. I doubt the puppy could have gone farther than that." I looked at my watch and thought, *I hope we're not too late.* "Let's meet here in thirty minutes."

The search lasted forty-five minutes. One after the other, the men returned. Their stories were the same. "We didn't find the pup."

Hugo, the night watchman, had left at 7:00 a.m., so I couldn't question him.

I found a workman who knew where Hugo lived and gave me his address. Knowing how poorly the locals identified their houses with street numbers, and the government's lack of interest in posting street signs, I set out to find Hugo. I wanted to know what, if anything, he knew about the pup's disappearance.

Driving along an almost nonexistent sand road, I found Hugo's so-called house. It was built from scrap sheet metal, varying sized pieces of plywood, and tar paper.

I knocked on his scrap-wood door and called out, "Hello. Anyone home?"

"Here," Hugo said, opening the door held by one hinge. "Come in out of the sun."

I entered the dark and cool one room home.

"Thanks," I said, shaking his hand. "Did you see the puppy this morning?"

"No," Hugo said, taking a swallow of Coca Cola. "Not this morning. I fed him two times last night. He took about an ounce of water each time. At about nine thirty, before I went to sleep, I checked on him. He looked okay . . . asleep under the woodpile. During the night, I didn't hear nothing unusual."

"Did you hear any dogs barking?"

"No, nothing. It was a quiet night."

Fearing Hugo might have had too many beers the evening before, I asked, "You weren't drinking last night were you?"

"No. Not even a beer. I can't afford beer this time of the month. Got no money."

"What time did you get up?"

"About seven. I went to feed the dog, but he wasn't there. I searched around the house but didn't see him anywhere. I got no idea where he went."

With a heavy heart, I left Hugo's house not knowing what to do. As I drove to the beach, I began a period of self-incrimination about what I could have done or perhaps what I should have done to protect the puppy before I left the night before. I thought, *I've failed the poor thing. Maybe he's dead, now.*

Beginning a pep-talk to myself, I thought, *Frank, you've done all you can do. You should feel good you had a chance to ease the puppy's last hours of suffering, but fate has taken its course. The puppy has gone off somewhere to die—hopefully in peace.*

I remembered hearing about canines that go to special places to die, something like the elephants' graveyard—but for dogs. I hoped the pup had died in peace, and the buzzards would not find him. I hated the thought of him being torn apart by those bastards' sharp beaks and talons.

At my construction site, the day's heat lingered. I busied myself with various tasks concerning work, but I could not rid myself of thoughts about the puppy. I had brief episodes of depression about what might have happened to the pup. I couldn't imagine how such a brief encounter with an animal could have touched me so deeply, but this little pup was so ill and defenseless I couldn't help but feel sad.

Got to shake off this sentimentality. It's reasonable.

My project engineer, Marco, called to me from behind the bedroom building where he had been working on a new project and wanted my input. I finished a discussion with a worker inside the front building then started across the courtyard to see what Marco wanted.

Midway of my trek across the courtyard, I saw the puppy wobble onto the construction site. He waddled toward the shady wood pile as fast as his scrawny little legs would carry him. He walked with a little more spunk than he had the day before. Perhaps the water and food, he had the previous day, had strengthened him.

Looking at the waiting engineer, Marco, I grinned, shook my fist in the air, and announced, "He's back! The puppy's back!"

Filled with unexpected happiness, I choked up.

Nearby workers, hearing me yell, stopped their work, looked in the direction of the puppy, and clapped.

I watched the puppy settle himself under the woodpile while I crossed the courtyard to consult with the waiting engineer.

"Go, take care of your puppy then come back," Marco said as he waved toward the woodpile.

"Thanks, but he can wait a moment, unless your problem is going to take a lot of time."

"I need you for just a moment," Marco said, turning to point at a problem hole in the floor.

We discussed options to solve the problem then chose the most expeditious solution.

"Okay," I said. "Let's get it done."

I went to get the treats, water, milk, and bowls

from the car then took them to the woodpile. I knelt to give the pup some broken bits of a dog treat.

The puppy seemed to accept my presence with less fear and shaking than the previous day. To my delight, he raised himself on his thin front legs then ate the food. Seconds later, fatigue set in. The puppy had to lie down to continue eating. While he ate, I poured water and milk in the bowls then pushed them toward him. He pulled himself up to a half-sitting position and lapped at the water then the milk. Having his fill, he curled into a ball of red, hairless flesh and fell asleep.

The veterinarian's office would not open until late afternoon, so I let the puppy sleep for the remainder of the day.

I felt a great sense of calm and relief knowing he had returned. He now had protection and access to water and food.

Late in the afternoon, I spread one of the cheap towels over a pillow I had borrowed from the hotel's sofa, which I placed on the front passenger seat of my car. I inserted the key in the ignition switch then went to get the puppy. He had just awakened.

I broke a dog-treat into small pieces then dropped them in a line from the woodpile toward the car's open right front door. I used small pieces for fear larger ones would fill his small belly, and he would stop short of the open door. I felt elated that the pup took the bait. Bit-by-bit, he ate his way toward the car.

While he ate, I donned rubber gloves then pulled the waiting second towel from the back waistband of my pants.

As the puppy consumed the last morsel, I draped

the second towel over his frail body then picked him

up, mid-bite. I startled him, but he managed to swallow the food. I couldn't decide if his squirming was from pain or the fact that he didn't like being picked up. I had concerns about how the texture of the towel might feel against his skin, but what were my alternatives?

Sometime you have to hurt a little in order to help, I thought.

I hoped I hadn't caused pain or discomfort as I placed the pup on the towel-covered pillow then closed the door. I bolted around the car, sat down on the driver's seat and then removed the rubber glove from my left driving hand.

The puppy seemed frightened.

This has to be the first time he's been in a car and the first time he's been penned in.

I started the engine then extended my gloved right hand toward the puppy to caress him, but then I wondered if my touch might be painful, so I didn't touch him. I drove away at five miles an hour, using only my left hand to steer.

The pup trembled as he stared up at me through slit-like eyelids. In an attempt to calm him, I spoke what I hoped were calming words.

During the drive, I caressed him. Much to my surprise, my touch was accepted.

Guess I'm not hurting him.

I whispered soft words, hoping to console him.

We rode over some very bumpy roads. Ninety-nine percent of Chuburna's roads are not paved. In fact, roads are nothing but compacted tire ruts in the area's ubiquitous sand. Because of that, I drove at ten miles an hour so not to alarm the pup with bumps and strange road sounds.

After a few blocks, I came to the only asphalt-covered road where I could drive faster. The puppy shivered and then looked at me through squinty eyes as if wondering 'what is next.'

The pillow on the puppy's seat made it possible to push himself up to the car's window ledge. With the assistance of quivering, spindly rear legs, he forced himself upright, placing one front paw on the arm rest and the other on the window ledge. I lowered his window, assuming he, like most dogs, wanted to sniff the air and feel the breeze. He did, but his chin just reached the opening. It remained on the window ledge for all of five seconds. After that, he tired and lost strength in his legs. The small sharp nails of his front paws helped him hold onto the window ledge and arm rest, but his front legs soon failed. His head sagged, causing him to lower his chin farther down the ledge where he continued to peer out the window.

I wondered what thoughts were going through his mind as he lived this new experience.

With growing fatigue, his front paws slid from the window ledge and onto the arm rest. His nails scraped down the door's surface as he lowered himself onto the towel-covered pillow where he slumped with a thud, curled into a ball, and then fell into a deep sleep. I directed the air conditioning vents away from his inflamed skin and covered him with one end of the towel. Except for shallow breathing, he remained motionless, lost in the sleep of exhaustion.

Twenty minutes later, we arrived at the veterinarian's office.

The office had once been a private home which blended in with the other nondescript homes on the street. All had faded paint and front porches where families could spend hot evenings in hammocks as the group watched television.

I tried to open the pup's door without waking him, but he awoke. He appeared confused. He appeared nervous as he looked around but remained quiet as I picked him up with the towel.

I rang the Puppy Palace doorbell then heard the vet yell from the back. "Come on back, Frank."

I made my way along a narrow hall to an examination room painted a bright pink.

"Hello Doctor. Thanks for seeing us."

The air was heavy with the odor of dog perfume used in an attempt to cover the odor of caged barking dogs and their waste farther back in the clinic.

"No problem," Dr. Beatrice said. "That's why I'm here. What's going on?"

The vet appeared to be of Mayan and Spanish heritage. Her black hair was iridescent and matched the brightness of her teeth exposed in a wide smile.

I placed the pup on the examination table where he trembled and leaked a few drops of urine.

"Sorry about the urine," I said.

"Don't worry," she said. "Urine is a good sign. It means his kidneys are functioning."

I tried to console the anxious puppy with gentle caresses, but that did not work. I wondered if the nearby barking dogs and crying cats had unnerved him.

The doctor said, "It's best if we simply proceeded with the examination. I'll be as gentle as I can." She probed the puppy then said, "He's suffering from severe malnutrition and intestinal parasites. He also has a water-filled abdominal cavity due to low blood protein. As for his skin, he has red mange and seconddary bacterial infections, anemia, conjunctivitis, and heart worms."

"Oh! That's all," I chuckled. "What caused the mange?"

"It's due to a parasite like in human scabies.

They invade hair follicles," she said, pointing to the web of skin between his first and second toe. "Your puppy probably got them from his mother. It's very common in local dogs." The vet moved her stethoscope aside so it could be cleaned before being used on a future patient. "Given all his problems, I believe he has only a few days of life expectancy—if treatment isn't started right away."

While I was not a vet, the gravity of the puppy's health status seemed obvious to me.

"Let's do what we can, "I said.

The pup's various internal conditions were treated with three injections and some force-fed pills.

The veterinarian handed me a prescription. "You should bathe the puppy with this shampoo every day for ten days. Feed him whatever he will eat."

My heart sank as I heard that *I* was to bathe the puppy—everyday.

Where am I to keep the puppy thoughts flashed through my mind.

"Doctor, I'm staying in a hotel that doesn't allow healthy dogs much less a sick one, and my worksite is no place for a sick puppy. My well water is not suitable for consumption and won't be until the treatment equipment is installed some eight to ten weeks from now. Would you please keep the puppy? I have no place to care for him."

She shrugged and said, "Sorry. I can't. I have a full house and no isolation cage for your puppy. He needs an isolation cage because his skin condition is contagious. I can't risk infecting the other dogs."

My heart not only sank; it fell to the floor.

What've I done? What've I gotten myself into? I've interfered with the natural death process of a sick puppy for naught.

I pleaded, "Please, I have no place to take him. I can't just let him die. I can't leave him alone at the beach. Please keep him. I'll pay whatever it takes."

"I can't," the vet said. "I'm sorry."

It seemed she hated to deny me help, so I continued to plead and beg for her assistance.

She apologized then said, "No." She turned, took a few steps, and then stopped. My persistent begging must have struck a deeply buried core of pity. "Let me call someone. See if I can borrow an isolation cage."

She opened her cellphone then dialed a number.

"Hello, this is Beatrice, at the Puppy Palace. I need an isolation cage. Do you have one I could borrow?"

After what seemed like a week of waiting for a reply, she said, "You do! That's wonderful. May I send for it?"

She turned to me, smiled, and then said, "It will be delivered in a few minutes."

Words could not describe the elation I felt, knowing the puppy would get the care he needed. He would live.

I informed the doctor that in three days, I had to travel to the United States and would return in three weeks. I would pay whatever it took for the puppy's treatment until I returned.

"Let me give you these *pesos* for the immediate care," I pleaded, holding out a 500 *peso* note.

"Don't' worry," she said, "pay me when you return."

"Thank you from the bottom of my heart. I'll be visiting every day, prior to my trip, to check on his progress."

The vet would have had a hard time keeping me away, but I also didn't want her to think I was going to abandon the puppy by saying I needed to travel.

The puppy was admitted to the Puppy Palace hospital and needed to be registered. This entailed giving him a name. Prior to that time, I had not considered naming the puppy. Naming him would have created bounds undesired at the time. My neglect of this formality had been a way of protecting me from having to grieve the puppy's presumed impending death.

After a few moments of thought, I decided to name him Chico.

The Spanish word *Chico* can be a noun or an adjective, depending on context. In its masculine form, it means "cute little boy." To me, the puppy was indeed Chico.

For the next three days, I visited Chico on my way to and from my construction site. Day-after-day, he ate and drank more like a healthy dog, growing stronger and stronger.

There were times when I thought he recognized me, but I often wondered if it was my doggy treats and not me that excited him. Nevertheless, his hair-less stub-of-a-tail wagged every time I approached his cage.

Despite his resolving skin condition, he enjoyed being caressed. We were bonding.

At my worksite, I inquired of the workers and a few neighbors as to where they thought the puppy might have come from. No one seemed to know.

One neighbor said, "He must have been born to a sick mother. I saw one limping around one of those boarded-up houses near your work site. I haven't seen her for days, and I don't know anything about puppies. Maybe the mother-dog is dead—had her puppies and then died."

As a feral animal, the sick mother-dog would have been ignored or chased from the neighborhood because she was pregnant and had a skin disease feared by villagers. Fear of contagion, plus unwanted

33

puppies, placed sick animals in jeopardy since any chance of them finding food or water without human assistance would be minuscule.

Having no other information, I assumed the recently sighted, sick mother-dog, with red mange similar to Chico's, had been Chico's mother. She had, no doubt, died of starvation or the diseases that plagued feral dogs. Chico had, no doubt, gotten his health problems from his now dead mother.

How eight-week old Chico found his way to my site has never been determined, but his presumed birthplace was about three-quarters of a mile east of my site. The miracle of it all was he was able to travel in his weakened state.

Three weeks after leaving Chico with the vet, I returned to Mexico. My first order of business was to visit him.

As I entered the basic animal hospital, I heard a cacophony of barking dogs and a cat that screeched like a dying child.

I hurried through the darkened front room, once a formal living room, then greeted the veterinarian working at her desk in the back part of the building. She smiled, rose, and we exchanged a continental kiss.

"I have great news," she said. "Chico is ninety percent better. Come, I'll show you."

We walked down a narrow corridor into an open courtyard covered with colorful, local handmade concrete "pasta tiles." Rows of stacked animal cages lined two walls of the open courtyard. Each occupant barked as we passed its cage. Within a minute, every dog barked so much I couldn't hear the vet speak as she pointed to Chico.

Chained, he rested on the floor outside his isolation cage. His skin appeared almost normal. He had regrown most of his hair, which was destined to be a very short coat. The color markings of his coat— brown and black spots—revealed themselves on a white coat. He had near-normal looking muscles on his legs, hip and shoulders girdles. His once bloated abdomen had shrunk. He no longer looked pregnant.

I could have sworn he had a smile. I know I did. My fears of his near-imminent demise vanished.

As I approached, he wagged his stubby tail as though it was being unscrewed. Filled with excitement, he jumped about and made happy, whining sounds. I knelt to rub and scratch his head, when in a flash, he licked my face. I offered him some dog treats, which he devoured. No doubt, he remembered them from three weeks earlier.

The veterinarian removed Chico's leash. "Let's let him run around the courtyard. He needs to stretch his legs."

The freed, excited dog circled me, jumping and whining as I sat down on a small stool in the shade of a mango tree and observed his play.

He struggled to get onto my lap, so I assisted him and then received another lick to my face. I cradled him in my arms and rubbed his belly. For a few minutes, he and I enjoyed our togetherness.

I put him onto the floor, reconnected his leash and collar then took my leave for the day. I was a most happy "daddy."

I informed the veterinarian, "I'll return tomorrow to take him home."

I visited my construction site and shared the good news about Chico's recovery with the workers. They surprised me with their unexpected excitement. The perceived non-dog-friendly workers seemed happy about his anticipated return and clapped when told the good news.

I spent the day thinking of how lucky Chico and I were to have found each other.

After the workday, I visited the equivalent of a Wal Mart store and purchased a doghouse, toys, and accessories needed for the new family member.

The next morning, I drove to the Puppy Palace and claimed Chico.

I lowered the car windows so he could stick his nose out, but he wanted nothing to do with the open window. Almost in a panic, he climbed everywhere, not knowing what to make of the closed space.

How different than his first ride.

I tried to calm him but to no avail. He climbed onto my lap and then put his head under my left arm-pit and shook.

Somehow, I managed to drive with my left hand while I stroked his neck and back with my right hand. I tried to avoid speed-bumps. Those I could not avoid, I drove over or around at three miles an hour, trying not to frighten him with abrupt movements.

After a few minutes into the drive, he calmed down, stretched out across my lap, and then went to sleep.

At the beach, Chico seemed apprehensive about leaving the car. Nevertheless, I placed him onto the sand where his anxiety vanished. His paws must have felt at home on the sand, for he ran all over the sandy yard. After all, he had been born and lived on sand. He ran with great vigor, smelling everything and everyone in sight. He had returned home.

Chico had been born housebroken. Not once did he abuse a manmade surface. When nature called, he always found his way to the "sandbox" somewhere in the front yard which was an enclosed extension of the beach.

He grew into adulthood and lived at the beach house where he became my resident watchdog.

Despite his traumatic puppyhood, he appeared to be the most contented dog in the world.

He was neutered and cannot add to the feral dog population, but that does not mean he does not try.

Chico has brought great pleasure not only to me but my *gringo* and Mexican friends as well.

When I returned to the U.S. for the summer, Chico was cared for by Hugo who became my fulltime caretaker-in-residence.

If a dog will not come to you after having looked you in the face, you should go home and examine your conscience.

Woodrow Wilson

Chapter 2

Where the Puppies Live

The previous and following stories are based on true experiences of feral dogs living in the State of Yucatan, Mexico. Readers would better appreciate their struggles if they knew about the socioeconomics of Yucatan, for the fate of these storied dogs is mirrored in the lives of local people. Few village dogs live beyond the age of two, and villagers live shorter lives than city peers.

Progreso, a port city on the northern coast of the Yucatan Peninsula, has a population of 25,000. It is a gritty town and home to friendly and welcoming people of mixed Mayan and Spanish heritage.

The city hosts several cruise ships during the winter months. Most passengers are bused to ancient Mayan sites or the colonial city of Merida—population one million.

Few village children attend school beyond the ninth grade. For this reason, most locals have low paying jobs, but that is changing as expats create scholarships, or provide domestic and construction employment. Most residents earn less than (US) $3,500.00 a year.

Maritime activities constitute the city's major industry. Second tier jobs are related to private individuals catching and selling fish, shellfish, and octopus. Third tier jobs involve manual labor, waiter services, and housekeeping. Many families operate small bars or cheap restaurants (cocinas economica) in their homes.

Fishing villages, east and west of Progreso, pose as summer beach-resorts. Middle class inhabitants of Merida have second homes here, most of which are boarded until summer. At that time, urbanites flee the city in search of cool ocean breezes as Merida temperatures reach 105° F.

On leaving any village's single asphalt road, drivers find themselves on sand roads. This is where most feral dogs live.

Village homes are small concrete block houses. One room often serves as: living room, dining room and bedroom. A room may sleep up to eight people using hammocks, the bedding of choice. Hammocks are cheap, take up little space, and are cooler than mattresses on hot, summer nights. When the hammocks are rolled and stowed in the morning, the bedroom becomes a living room again.

Village yards are small, sandy walled in plots, without grass, often containing coconut palms that bear fruit year-round. Coconut meat is used to make custards and pies often sold at family-operated roadside stands.

Skillet-fried tortillas, eaten with fish or eggs, are staples. Cheap cuts of beef and pork are enjoyed by families with more disposable income. Turkey frankfurters are regular meat substitutes. Green vegetables are not popular or easy to grow in sandy gardens.

Many village men will fish half the year if a government permit is available. Unfortunately, overfishing has reduced fish populations. When men cannot fish, they work for foreigners, building or renovating homes. Other men work as handymen while waiting for a "real" job.

"Wealthy" construction workers own a single speed bicycle. Owners charge ten to twenty cents to allow a fellow worker stand on the bicycle's extended rear axle as the owner pedals toward a worksite.

Bicycles are void of mirrors, fenders, lights or reflectors. Sooner or later, most bicyclists will be involved in an accident with cars—the major cause of death of villagers under the age of twenty-five. Roadsides are dotted with shrines marking the spot where someone died.

Worker's "uniforms" consist of cheap, cotton shorts, flip-flops, baseball hats and t-shirts—often displaying local beer, or cola logos. Workers have no gloves, goggles, or steel-toed shoes to protect against work injuries. Expats who provide gloves and safety goggles often find laborers don't use the items.

Physicians can be a rarity in villages. So-called EMTs have little medical equipment. Several villages share an ambulance service consisting of one vehicle that may have to travel many miles to respond to an emergency.

Few villagers have health insurance—costing about (US) $300.00 per year. Most sick and injured locals go to public hospitals or clinics where they may wait hours for care. Government budgets often don't cover needed medications.

Air-conditioning is all but unnecessary between mid-October and May, when the temperature range is 72-78 degrees Fahrenheit. However, summer humidity and heat warrants air conditioning. However, most homes have no air conditioning. On hot nights, locals move their hammocks to porches for alfresco sleeping.

Zocálos (town squares) function as political, social, entertainment, religious, and dining venues.

Festivals attract modest carnivals whose equipment has had little maintenance. Their paint is faded or flaking, and rust can be seen on every moving part.

Frayed electrical wires, bruised by masses of strolling feet, cover carnival grounds like rivers of snakes, yet no one seems concerned about electrocution.

Marginally safe, carnival rides are affordable. Snacks and soft drinks (*frescas)* are cheap. The sparkle of lights, loud music, and crowd-generated excitement is free.

On religious holidays, processions of devout Catholics, mostly elderly men and women, snake along sandy roads. Devotees carry statutes of the Blessed Virgin or other saint *du jour* and are followed by school bands whose almost in tune, loud martial musical talents are counterbalanced with enthusiasm and off-key notes. Celebrants shuffle along uttering the soft murmurings of Hail Marys.

Once a year, fishermen place a statue of the Blessed Mother on a boat then parade her image along the shore as a Catholic priest blesses the ocean, boats, and fishermen while praying for fishermen's safety.

Beggars are rare in villages, and no one starves. In fact, most residents seem overfed. They eat at home or in *cocinas economica* or in a few commercial restaurants serving fried fish.

Liters of Coca Cola are a staple of the diet along with fried fish, a few homegrown fruits, tomatoes, onions, and chili peppers. Beer is cheap beer and available in restaurants and state licensed outlets. Occasionally, a chronic alcoholic is seen wandering local streets, waiting for someone to offer them a beer or a menial job to earn enough *pesos* to purchase a beer.

The average family owns no pets. If they do, it is most often a male dog. Males don't bear offspring and cost less to neuter—if neutering is even considered. Many Mexican men consider it unmanly to neuter a male dog. Neutering costs the equivalent of two or three days' wages for a villager.

It is rumored, officials sometime distribute rat poison where packs of stray animals congregate. Poison is less expensive than neutering, capture-and-hold, or capture-and-kill programs. Because the animal dies from internal hemorrhaging, there is no "mess" when the animal dies.

Villagers are reluctant to feed or provide water to stray dogs because they might take up residence, bring diseases, or deliver unwanted pups.

Pregnant and sick animals are driven away from towns. Deprivation forces these outcasts into scavenging—a frantic day-to-day search for anything to kill hunger.

Starvation causes dogs' bloated abdomens similar to the starving children of Darfur seen on television. Bloated bellies are due to low blood protein levels.

Intestinal worms cause "internal" starvation where the parasite ingest food before it can be absorbed by the dog's intestines.

Ticks and fleas can cause death from associated bacterial infections and anemia due to "drinking" the animal's blood.

Heartworms, spread by mosquitos, are also a problem for dogs. These worms can cause heart failure and death by blocking blood flow. Treatment may be as dangerous for the dog as the parasites.

It is against this socioeconomic and cultural background that these stories are written.

Progreso veterinarian Doctor Beatrice Garcia has

played a major role in the lives of several puppies that star in the short stories contained in this book. As you read about these Yucatican dogs, I hope you will come to love and sympathize with their peers as do I.

Chapter 3

Chica

I could not have imagined how the events of that Sunday would affect my life. The day would see the gathering of friends, good food, drinks, laughter, and heartache.

On that particular February Sunday, a new friend would attend a house party at my beach house. He had to leave early invited me to stop by his nearby condo after my party ended. I accepted his invitation.

At 4:00 p.m., I began a relaxing stroll along the beach toward his beachfront building. His condo was in the only high-rise building in Chuburna and stood one kilometer west of my house.

The late afternoon sky, a perfect shade of bird-egg blue, had a few clouds that blocked the searing heat of the sun.

Ninety percent of the houses along the beach were boarded up until they would be opened by their owners in May or June, so they could escape the heat and humidity of Merida thirty miles south. However, during *Semana Santa*, or Easter Holy Week, many Yucaticans celebrate a two-week holiday period centered on Easter Sunday when the beach would be packed with thousands of people in a party mood. This was not the case on the Sunday of my party. Other than a few of my guests, no one else walked the beach.

With sandals dangling from my hand, my feet delighted in the cool sand at water's edge. The gusting breezes, wafting off the Gulf of Mexico, felt wonderful. Periodically, I had to push my straw hat onto my head to prevent it from being blown away.

What a great day to be alive! I thought, watching waves lap the shore while palm trees swayed.

After walking several blocks, I turned left and stepped onto a sand-road. This road and my friend's building were separated by an eight-foot-high wall that extended southward from the Gulf. A gated driveway opened at the southern end of the wall. Just beyond the end of the wall stood a boarded-up house, waiting for the return of its owner.

I whistled as I walked toward the driveway. Ahead, I saw some unusual motions in the weeds which blanketed most of the front yard of the vacant house. Being curios, I approached the moving weeds.

Much to my surprise, two black puppies pushed their way through the tall, dry growth and waddled toward me. Behind the black pups lagged a beige puppy—its gait slow and shaky.

The pups appeared to be about eight weeks old. Each black pup had a small clump of white hair between their eyes. One had a wisp of white chin whiskers. These almost solid black-coated dogs were quite unusual in Chuburna Puerto where most dogs' coats were a mix of browns, reds, and creams.

The beige puppy had what I thought were a few, narrow bands of lighter coloration over its left and right ribcage. As I pondered the stripes, I realized the light colorations were not normal.

"Oh my god," I mumbled. "The puppy has mange."

As I delighted in the sight of the puppies, Ian, a friend who had been invited to the same apartment as I, approached. He too noticed the puppies.

"Hello," I said, shaking Ian's hand. "Looks like a puppy den here."

"They're cute." he said.

"They're darling. But hey, I've never seen an ugly puppy, but I have a weakness for puppies. By the way, how are your city dogs doing?"

"Oh, they're grown now and into everything. But don't get too close to these pups," Ian said. "They're probably covered with fleas and ticks."

"Yeah, but aren't they cute?"

We watched the puppies for a few moments. The black puppies were more brazen than the beige one. Approaching our shoes, the pups wanted petting, but they also whined the whine of hunger and loneliness.

"Do you think they're hungry?" I asked.

Ian nodded. "Knowing this part of the world and the villager's lack of concern for dogs, you bet they're hungry. Have you seen the mother?"

"No yet, but I got here only a minute before you arrived. There were no adult dogs around."

"You can bet they're abandoned," Ian said, waving his hands dismissingly.

I extended my hand toward the nearest black pup. Instead of stopping to be scratched or get a pat to the head, the puppy sucked my fingertip. On closer inspection, I could see the puppies were very thin—starved thin. Their black coats camouflaged their state of starvation and bloated bellies—common to feral dogs in the Yucatan.

"Look how thin their coats are," I said, pushing

one pup's hair against the grain.

"That's common. Make sure you wash your hands as soon as you get in David's place. You never know what diseases these dogs have."

"You bet I will!"

I noted each puppy was infected with mange, causing some spotty hair loss. *Thank God; they don't have total loss of hair.*

The timid beige puppy retreated to the house where it found a shady spot. I crept toward it, hoping not to spook it. After a moment of visual inspection, I knew the puppy had several health problems, no doubt the same as its siblings except this one seemed worse. It panted as if exhausted from something other than heat.

"Too bad there are so many sick dogs in this area," Ian said. "I hate to see them living like this, but I can't get involved. I already have two rescued dogs at home."

"And don't you forget, I too have a rescued dog. I know they're a big commitment, but I can't just ignore these puppies. At eight weeks of age they already have bloated bellies. I bet their mother was starved all the time she carried them."

"Probably," Ian said, "but we had better get going."

"Yeah, David must be wondering what has happened to us."

Ian and I continued to discuss the sad state of affairs for feral animals. Entering the condominium complex, we made our way to our friend's apartment.

David invited us in, and then I washed my hands.

We went onto a balcony overlooking the Gulf where we had Mexico's classic drink—a Margarita. For much of the visit, we and other guests discussed the puppies and the problem of feral dogs.

50

Two hours later, David's social event ended. Ian and I left together.

We walked toward the boarded home where the grass-hidden puppies could be heard whining. When they saw us, they waddled our way.

"Listen to those poor things," I said. "They've got to be very thirsty. Who knows how long it's been since they had anything to eat or drink?"

"I don't hear anything," Ian said, placing his fingers in his ears.

I yelled, "They're thirsty."

"Sorry, I can't hear you." Ian smiled then said, "Whatever. I've got to hustle. I parked three blocks away so I wouldn't get stuck in the loose sand I encountered the last time I was here. I fear getting stuck in the damn stuff." He turned to walk away and said, "Talk to you later."

"You do what you have to," I said, "but I can't just walk away. I'm going home to get some milk and water for these guys. I have to feed them."

"Do what you want, but I'm not getting involved with any more dogs," Ian yelled from half a block away. "I'm out of here. You want a lift?"

"No thanks. I'd be half way home by the time I walked to your car."

I bid Ian *adieux* and hurried home to get the bowl that I had used in the rescue of Chico a year earlier. There was some bottled water and a carton of milk in my refrigerator that could be used in caring for the pups.

As I exited my car, the puppies waddled toward me, struggling against the thick weeds.

Behind me, I heard voices from a house across the street from the puppy's home. Curious, I headed to the house and asked, "Do you know anything about

51

the puppies at your neighbor's house?"

A short, rotund man rose from his white plastic chair as I approached. "No. They just turned up a few days ago."

"Anyone recall seeing their mother?" I asked.

"No," the man replied. "We think the puppies were dropped off by somebody that didn't want more dogs."

From her hammock, a next-door neighbor yelled, "The mother might have had 'em somewhere around the house and then died of who knows what. Maybe she got poisoned or hit by a car."

Sadly, the neighbor knew of the puppies' plight but had refused to get involved. Perhaps they didn't because they already owned one dog that slept in the shade of the porch. Perhaps, its owner didn't want another dog, so he left the puppies to die.

Whatever had happened to the mother dog, she had not been seen. It seemed the puppies had not been fed in many days and also suffered from dehydration.

One neighbor, walking into her house, said, "I think the beige one is very sick."

I thought, *She must have looked in on them otherwise she wouldn't know that.*

I walked into the lengthening shadow of the boarded house the puppies knew as home. Onto the shaded sand, I placed a bowl then filled it with water. The puppies scrambled to the bowl and lapped at the liquid.

Wow! From the way these guys attacked that water I don't think they've had any in days.

The black puppies nudged the smaller, weaker beige puppy from the bowl. When it moved to another spot at the rim, the other pups dislodged the weaker one time after time. Fatigued from fighting, the ousted pup waddled four feet from the drinking pups and collapsed, belly down, under the house.

52

Knowing the beige pup needed water, I picked up the bowl then placed it in front of the reclusive pup. She rolled submissively onto her back, tucked her bony, hairless tail against her abdomen where it shook from side-to-side. The puppy's belly swarmed with more fleas than I had ever seen. They scrambled over each other to get to an unclaimed spot of skin on which to feed. There were many infected flea bites and pustules scattered over her abdomen and in the creases of skin in her "arm" pits.

I feared getting close to the pups for fear the fleas would hitch a ride on me. Nevertheless, I picked up the beige pup and placed her on her feet. Her tail remained tucked between her legs and quivered.

I pushed the water bowl close to her mouth. She first sniffed the bowl and then drank. I examined my hands and arms to make sure I had not acquired any fleas. As she lapped at the water, I couldn't help notice the color of her tongue—white.

What breed of dog has a white tongue?

Dogs should have a dark pink or red tongue except for the Chinese Chow, which has a dark-purple tongue.

I don't recall any breed that has a white tongue.

Suddenly, it dawned on me. The fleas had drained the wretched pup's blood. Her tongue was not genetically white but white due to blood loss. The fleas were "drinking" the last of the puppy's blood.

That's why she moves so slowly.

I interrupted her drinking to press my fingertip against her upper gum. She resisted, but I persisted. A normal gum would have blanched from red to pale pink as the pressure of my fingertip temporally halted the gum's blood flow. Once I removed my finger, the gum's red color should have returned in a second or two. However, my pressing caused *no* change in color. Now, I was certain why she moved so slowly.

She had anemia and was "running on empty" in regard to blood volume. She needed the human equivalent of eight pints of transfused blood.

Little puppy, you are in serious trouble.

The black puppies waddled toward the water bowl, but I held them back until the beige female could satisfy her thirst. Having done so, the other puppies were permitted to drink. As the black puppies drank, the beige pup withdrew to a spot just under the edge of the house. She seemed to prefer that location in times of stress.

The black pups were allowed to drink a little longer, but I didn't want them to consume too much too quickly for fear of causing additional health problems. I dumped the remaining water onto the sand. One puppy started to lick the wet sand.

"No! Don't lick that," I yelled at the pup.

It shouldn't ingest wet sand. It could plug its GI tract.

The pup was startled by my outburst and gave up its interest in wet sand.

I poured milk into the bowl then first presented it to the beige female and later to the other puppies. All drank as if they were starved. No doubt, they were. After a minute, I stopped their gluttonous feeding. Too much milk at one time could cause other problems.

I wondered what I should do to help these little fur balls. My first thought, get them cleaned up. God knew they needed a bath and defleaing.

I soon decided on a plan: purchase anti-flea shampoo, search for a cardboard transport-box, and then return to the puppy den the following day. I would transport the boxed puppies to my house. There I could bathe, shampoo, feed and water them, and then take them to my veterinarian. After they were treated and on the mend, I would return them to the spot where I found them. There, I would provide them with daily feedings and water until they were strong enough to fend for themselves.

I kept telling myself that I had to remain emotionally detached throughout this process if my plan

was to have a chance of working. However, something about the beige pup had caught my eye—and heart. Perhaps her vulnerability and state of utter helplessness had stirred my sympathy. Despite my trying to push such thoughts from my mind, I could not help but entertain the possibility that she might be kept as a companion for my Chico, the rescue-dog at home.

I drove to the *bodega* in Progreso where I stopped at the service desk. The lone woman at the desk nodded. Her name tag read, Carmen.

She smiled then said, "*Buenos tardes*."

"*Habla Ingles*," I asked.

"*Si*," she replied. "A little."

I felt relieved because I didn't speak very much Spanish. I informed Carmen about the puppies and my need of a cardboard box.

Carmen smiled, adjusted her uniform's upper button and said, "I love dogs. My son has one. Her name is Frieda. She got her name from another dog we had. It died last year." Carmen looked at the floor, took a deep breath, and then continued. "She and my son had bonded like glue. Where you saw one, you saw the other."

"Yeah," I said. "I know how easy it is to get attached to dogs. I have a mini Dachshund, Greta, back in the States. She's fifteen years old. I also have a dog here. I rescued him last year."

"Keep me posted on how your puppies are doing," Carmen said and then giggled. "Maybe I can convince my husband to take in another dog as a companion for Frieda."

Carmen picked up the public-address microphone and paged a service person. When he arrived, Carmen asked him to bring three boxes, of varying sizes, to the service desk.

"Carmen," I asked, "can you direct me to where I can find anti-flea shampoo?"

"Yes," she said, turning toward a clerk who was passing. "Maria, would you escort this customer to the pet department." Realizing the clerk didn't speak English, Carmen repeated her request in Spanish. She turned to me and said, "When you have everything you and your pups need, bring the items to the service desk."

"Thanks."

Carmen smiled. "By the time you get back, I will have some boxes for you."

I found the pet shampoo area. Unfortunately, the store had only one brand and its label did not disclose if it was safe for puppies. Having no alternatives, I took it to the service desk where boxes awaited my selection.

Holding an empty Clorox box in the air, Carmen asked, "What about this one? It should be big enough to carry three puppies."

"I think you're right." I forced my thumb into the cardboard. "It's strong and deep enough to keep the little critters inside. I'll take it."

I placed the shampoo on the service counter then reached for my wallet.

"That won't be necessary," Carmen said. There's no charge. Good luck with the puppies. I hope they do well."

Feeling happy, I said, "*Muchas gracias.* "I repeated in English. "Thank you."

I left the store with my gifts thinking, *Who says*

there's no such thing as "puppy love?"

The next morning, I drove to the puppy den at the boarded-up house. I anticipated a quick roundup of puppies and then transport home for the "defleaing process."

One of the black puppies and the beige puppy approached me. The black puppy had vigor, but the beige one moved like a snail. As always, the beige pup lagged several steps behind her sibling.

The second black puppy was nowhere to be seen. *Damn. Where the hell is that dog?*

I searched under the house for the missing puppy while three neighbors gathered and inquired about the animals.

I told them, "I plan to take the puppies to my house for a bath and then to the vets."

The neighbors seemed happy with the plan. Perhaps, I had relieved them of guilt for not having assisted the pups. I commented about not finding the third puppy.

"Will you help me search?" I asked.

"*Sí*. My pleasure," two men and a woman responded.

I welcomed their help. Soon, we were on "all fours" peering under buildings and bushes in search of the third pup.

An older woman, wearing a traditional white-cotton dress whose hem was covered with a colorful plethora of embroidered flowers, joined the search. It dragged in the sandy soil and risked being damaged, but the woman continued her search on all fours.

For fifteen minutes, we searched areas we thought the puppy might have wandered into, but the pup's location eluded us.

Saddened at not finding the pup, I decided to leave with two puppies. I wanted to believe someone had taken pity on the third pup and given it a forever home.

I got the box from my car, folded the top-flaps inside the container, grabbed an old towel, and then headed back to collect the pups.

With my towel-wrapped hand, I picked up the beige puppy then placed her in the box. Next, I retrieved the black pup and noted I had a second female. I placed her in the box with her sister. The puppies didn't know what to make of the box's slick bottom. They were accustomed to walking on coarse sand—not cardboard. They slipped every time they took a step. I spread the crumpled towel over the bottom of the carton for cushioning and better footing. The view-blocking sides of the box must have felt threatening to them because they whined within seconds of being placed inside.

Trying to calm the pups with almost whispered words, I carried the box to the car where I placed it on the passenger's seat. I waved goodbye to the neighbors and then drove away.

Accompanied by the disconcerting sounds of upset puppies, I headed toward our common destiny.

At home, I placed the box in a shady area near an outdoor faucet where the bathing would take place. Whines of protest from the box continued as I attempted to set the proper water temperature for the bath.

I ran four inches of water into a plastic container, added anti-flea shampoo until a thick layer of suds covered the surface, and then I donned my rubber gloves.

The beige female was first to be bathed. Due to her frailty, I took my time lowering her into the warm water. Her head cleared the suds, but she didn't like being wet. Despite her weakness, she tried to climb out of the container. Thinking the slippery bottom might be adding to her wariness, I lifted her half-out of the water. She complained with a weak whine then quieted down. I hand-cupped small amounts of sudsy water over her back and neck then worked the lather into her sparse coat—down to where the fleas had dug in. I stroked then massaged her back in an effort to remove the fleas and calm the nervous puppy.

Next, I used a fingertip to ferry suds into her ears where an army of fleas had taken up a defensive position. Soon, swimming—and I hoped drowning—fleas covered the sudsy water like soot on three-day-old city snow.

All at once, she stopped squirming. I hoped she appreciated being freed of fleas, but it is more likely she was simply tired.

The bath was repeated to make sure I had rid the pup of most, if not all, her fleas. I wanted to drain her pustules because I feared their toxins might lead to a generalized blood infection. With gentle compression, I drained them into the bath water.

I removed the puppy from the water then emptied the flea-infested water down a drain. I refilled the container, added shampoo to create more suds and then lowered the puppy back into the fresh, sudsy water. After three minutes of shampooing, I held the suds-dripping puppy under the gentle flow of the faucet's warm water and rinsed the suds from her frail body. She physically protested as I washed her face.

I called to Hugo, my caretaker, "Spread a towel under the puppy so I can dry her."

I dried the scrawny animal's coat as she struggled to get free.

"Hugo," I called, "will you please get me another towel?"

I continued to dry the puppy until Hugo returned with a fresh towel.

"Thanks," I said. "Take this wet one to the laundry room. I want these puppy-towels to be washed as a separate load. Tell Maria to use lots of bleach."

I completed the drying process then placed the pup on the patio. Mustering her energy, she forced herself erect on her tiny paws, and then in typical, innate dog-fashion, she attempted to shake herself dry. After one, mighty expenditure of energy, she toppled over. Having regained her balance, she sniffed and explored the patio whereupon she had a small bowel movement.

While Hugo picked up the mess, I filled the plastic container with water and shampoo for bathing the black puppy. I removed her from the box then gave her the same gentle care I had given her sister. The black pup, however, didn't mind being bathed. On the contrary, I had to stop her from licking the suds—another possible cause of an intestinal upset.

Soon the surface of the bath water rippled with dying fleas. They weren't, however, as numerous as from the beige pup. I emptied and then refilled the container with fresh water and shampoo for a second bath. As the second bath proceeded, I explored her ear canals, and much to my surprise, I found no fleas.

Rinsing, toweling, and the innate shaking-dry action terminated the bath. The bathed puppies then explored the patio, sniffing every inch of its surface.

As Hugo tried to offer a caress, they scampered into a near-by corner where they cowed and shook with fear.

"I think they are more afraid of you than of me," I said.

"Guess they don't like Mexicans," Hugo said then walked away.

I asked myself, *How should I bed these pups for the night?*

In broken Spanish, I yelled, "Hugo, what should we do with the puppies for the night?"

"Why not put the box on its side and use it as a doghouse?" he replied.

"I thought of that, but I don't think they'll stay Inside. I don't want them roaming all over the patio.

They'll make a mess, for sure." I stared at the box for a moment. "Let's turn the box on its side. That'll convert it into a doghouse. Then we put a towel on the side of the box. Uh, I mean the 'floor' of the doghouse."

"Okay," Hugo said, turning the box on its side.

"We'll need to build some barriers to keep them confined. Check behind the *casita* for boards."

"I'll check," Hugo said, leaving to search.

I corralled the dogs as Hugo went in search of boards. He soon returned with four planks that we used to construct a temporary corral around the doghouse, which sat in a corner of the walled terrace. I filled the dog's bowls with milk and water then placed them inside the barrier.

Suddenly, I thought about all the pee and poop that might accumulate on the terrace until the pups were taken to the vets the next day.

"Hugo, this isn't going to work."

"Why not?"

"If we keep the puppies here, *someone* will be busy cleaning up poop, and you know who that will be. We've got to come up with another option."

"Then move everything to the front yard."

My front yard is an extension of the beach. The puppies had been living, perhaps born, on sand, and I knew puppy poop would be easier to remove from sand than from patio concrete. The choice didn't require debate. The makeshift doghouse and puppies would be relocated to the front yard. I knew the pups

61

could be comfortable on the sand.

"Hugo, I'll take the pups; you bring the box and towel. Put it in the shadow of the palm trees."

I tossed the towel-bedding inside the relocated doghouse then placed the puppies on the towel.

"Let's stand back," I said. "See what happens."

At first, the pups smelled around the doghouse and the towel. In time, both pups moved out of the box onto the sand. They seemed to prefer its texture as they milled about smelling and exploring their new habitat. Even though the beige pup crept along, I felt relieved when I saw she had enough energy and inquisitiveness to want to explore her new home.

Chico, my resident watchdog and rescue, had returned home. He pondered the creatures roaming in *his* front yard. He sniffed them and then backed away, appearing puzzled. He turned his head one way and then another occasionally staring at me as if to ask, "What are these things doing here?"

I could see the puppies didn't like Chico's presence. His size and demeanor threatened them. After a few minutes of sniffing the pups, Chico lay motionless in the sand and stared in the puppies' direction. One-by-one, the puppies found their way to his side where they snuggled against his belly.

I wondered if they had confused him for their mother, maybe their father, or they simply wanted a warm place to sleep.

I asked myself, *Did they even know their father?*

Their snuggling seemed such a tender moment that I wanted to capture it.

I got my camera and then hurried back to the puppy-arena. I took several photos of the puppies and their interaction with Chico. Months later, I would be forever happy I had captured those magic moments of puppyhood.

For a moment, Chico lay motionless on his side

then turned his head toward the black pup and began to smell her in a typical dog-greeting fashion. The pup tensed, stood, and tucked her tail. Chico then sniffed the standing beige pup. The nudge of his nose caused the puppy to topple onto her side. She was frightened and cowered for a second. Each pup then ambled away, in opposite directions, stretched, coiled up on the sand, and descended into slumber's solace.

Twenty minutes later, the pups stirred. I got milk and bowls from the kitchen then placed them halfway between the two puppies. I retreated to the front porch to monitor the pup's intake.

They waddled to the bowls where the black puppy lapped the milk. The frail sister sniffed the milk then waddled into the doghouse where she curled up as if going to sleep but didn't. Her small, dark eyes glazed over as she stared blindly into space. She settled into the towels as if poured onto the bedding. She lay still, except for shallow breaths, oblivious to her surroundings.

Chico had been asleep on the porch but was awakened by the sounds of milk being lapped by the black pup. Chico galloped to the milk bowl and growled as if the milk belonged to him. The black puppy backed away, tail tucked under her belly.

Chico's aggression couldn't be allowed, so I restrained him and called to Hugo who worked nearby. "Take Chico to the back patio and put him on his leash. He's frightening the puppies."

I wondered if Chico might harm or kill one or both of the puppies as wild lions kill offspring sired by another father. I was also concerned he might "catch" some of the puppy's health problems. He had to be restrained until the pups could be taken to the clinic the next day.

As soon as Chico had been taken from the area, the black puppy approached the bowl then lapped at the milk. I pushed the milk bowl toward the doghouse, hoping both animals would claim the box as their temporary home and the beige pup might drink some of the milk.

The black puppy followed her food source. The beige pup lay motionless, staring at her approaching sister. I had growing apprehensions about the beige pup's lack of interest in milk or water, so I moved the water bowl closer to the doghouse then retreated to the front porch. From that location, I could observe the puppies' actions without being intrusive.

The black puppy continued to lap at the milk, but the beige puppy moved deeper into the doghouse, curled up on the towel, and then slept. The black pup drank all the milk then went into the doghouse where she curled around her frail sister. Soon, both puppies were asleep.

I fixed myself a Margarita then returned to the porch to watch the puppies. Both were awake. The black puppy moved with more spring in her step than her sister who remained curled. The beige pup was badgered a bit by the playful antics of the black pup. The beige pup didn't want to play. In fact, she appeared not to want to be bothered. Nevertheless, her sister persisted in gentle, but assertive, moves toward and over the smaller pup that recoiled from each playful lunge. I sensed the beige puppy wanted to be left alone.

The black pup had suddenly gotten too rambunctious for the good of her sister.

They've got to be separated.

"Hugo," I yelled, "please bring that plastic container I used to bathe the dogs?"

In a few minutes, Hugo arrived with the plastic box. "Sorry to take so long," he said. "I had to find a towel to dry it."

"Thanks. I want to see if it can be used as a dog bed."

I took the plastic box to the front yard and placed it beside the cardboard doghouse. I removed the towel from the box then placed it in the plastic container.

I placed the beige puppy on the towel. At first, she tried to escape the container, but with a gentle push of my hand, she lay on the towel and then went to sleep.

Using simple play tactics, I distracted the black puppy from bothering her sister. Soon the black pup tired of playing, and I left her to rest on the sand. Disliking solitude, the black puppy approached the plastic container and attempted to climb in. With some struggling, she made it into the container where she pounced on her sleeping sister in search of someone with whom to play.

For the physical safety of the beige pup, the sisters had to be separated. In an effort to keep everyone happy and safe, I placed the beige pup on the towel in the up righted cardboard box and let the black puppy roam freely on the sand. The smaller pup seemed relieved to be free of the playful attacks from her bigger sister.

With another towel inside, I placed the plastic container on its side, making it easier for the black pup to access it as her new home.

I sipped my Margarita, read a few magazines, and enjoyed the sea breeze and quietude of my front yard "neighbors" as the black pup also slept.

Two hours later, I offered another bowl of milk to the pups. I lifted the beige pup out of her box, placed her on the sand, and then nosed her toward the milk. She wanted nothing to do with it, but her sister lapped at it with abandon.

Hmmm, Beigeee won't take the milk. Maybe she'll take some water.

I nudged the beige pup's nose toward the water, but she rejected it. Concerned that she continued to refuse milk and water, I wondered what my next step should be. I knew she wouldn't survive much longer without nutrition and hydration.

What could I do to entice her to drink? Perhaps sweetening the liquids would help, so I placed a few drops of honey in a small amount of water and then into the bowl of milk. I offered the bowls to the pup and held my breath. She sniffed each but refused to drink from either.

Frustrated, I dipped my fingertip into the honey flavored milk then forced it into the pup's mouth. She didn't like having her mouth pried open, and she definitely did not want the milk. She tried to pull her head away and used her tongue to force my finger from her mouth. Nevertheless, I repeated the process using honey-flavored water. Again, she was disinterested.

My concerns were growing because she had not urinated. No urine probably meant that dehydration or renal failure had set in.

As evening approached I felt the need to catch up on my sleep deficit. Pulling the sheets to my chin, I consigned the puppies to the hands of God.

Before my morning coffee finished brewing, I went to see how the pups had fared during the night.

The black pup roamed around sniffing the sand. I knew she had taken a substantial amount of liquids because the water and milk levels in her bowls were low. She had also had a poop. I felt a lot better about the black puppy's health.

The beige pup lay quietly in her box, eyes closed. She breathed with a slow, steady rhythm, but the breaths were shallow. Instead of being curled into a ball, she had stretched out on her right side, each leg extended. This had not been her favorite position in the past and suggested something gone wrong.

"Hello little puppy," I said, stroking her side with one finger. "How are you doing?"

I watched her thin ribs move ever-so-slightly apart then come together. She half-opened her eyes but didn't move. After a few more caresses, she closed her eyes. I detected no change in fluid levels in either of the two bowls I had left for her the previous evening.

My heart filled with sadness, for I knew the pup had crossed an ominous threshold—perhaps death was closer than I had thought. pup needed a vet— right away, and I knew I couldn't wait until the afternoon appointment. I found the vet's telephone number then dialed it with a trembling hand. After seven rings, the vet answered.

"Doctor. This is Frank. I have an appointment to see you this afternoon, but one of my puppies is very sick. Could you see us right away?"

"Yes, by all means. Come now."

I dressed, gathered the pups, placed them in the cardboard box, and then headed for the vet's office.

The ride seemed to take forever. Even though I drove faster than the speed limit, time dragged. I en-countered all kinds of hindrances along the way: a slow-moving school bus, which one almost never sees in the Yucatan; small jitney buses that did not to pull to the side of the road to pick up or discharge passen-gers, making legal passing of the bus impossible; a horse drawn wagon, on wobbly wheels, moved at a snail's pace, in the middle of the road, and a group of bicyclists who commandeered the width of the road, refusing to move out of the way.

After what seemed a light year, I reached Progreso and snaked my way through the maze of one-way streets to the vet's office. I grabbed the box of puppies then hurried into the clinic where the vet waited.

"Would you please examine this one first?" I asked, holding up the beige pup. "She's very sick. I'm afraid she's dying."

"Let's have a look," the vet said.

Too weak to stand, the beige puppy seemed to melt onto the examination table.

The vet examined the pup as she asked, "How long have you had her?"

"About eighteen hours."

"Has she had anything to eat or drink?"

"She drank some water and a small amount of milk about twenty-four hours ago, but she has refused everything since then. She had a small pee and a poop about fifteen hours ago, but I haven't seen her pee since then."

"Has she been active?"

"Not very. For the past twenty-four hours, she has just stared into space."

After a few minutes, the vet said, "You're right. She is very ill. I doubt she'll survive her many problems. She is very dehydrated—maybe in renal failure. She is very anemic and maybe septic due to the infected flea bites. I'd say she has intestinal parasites as well."

Even though I dreaded hearing the truth, the information didn't surprise me. "Do whatever you need to do to save her," I said. I hoped—thought—*a nasogastric tube or intravenous fluids.*

When I inquired about these things, the vet said, "Such things are not available in this area."

My heart stopped for a second.

68

"Frank, don't forget you're in Mexico. Mexicans aren't as willing to spend money for pet care as you Americans. Village pet owners don't expect, or ask for, expensive care. If a pet is seriously ill, it's put to sleep."

My heart fell to my shoes as I dropped my head.

"I'll do everything I can," the vet said, "given my resources."

I think she sensed my anxiety as she said, "I'll force feed her, if I have to. If we can get just a small amount of water in her, that'll help a lot. We'll try every four hours."

"Okay," I murmured, not feeling too confident about a rescue. I had hoped for a more American-style approach to care.

The vet called to an assistant. When she arrived, the vet held out the puppy. "Take her to the back and force feed her some water."

My heart ached as the puppy was carried away.

The doctor examined the black puppy then spouted off a list of diagnoses that I had heard months earlier in regard to my Chico. All the mentioned diagnoses were common to feral dogs in Yucatan.

"This pup is a lot healthier than the beige one," the vet said, examining the restive black puppy.

"Seems that way to me."

"I think she'll do just fine. You've started her off on the right foot. She doesn't appear to be too dehydrated and she's very active."

At that moment, the black puppy peed on the examining table.

"Uupps. Sorry," I said, reaching for a roll of paper towels.

"Don't worry," the vet chuckled. "It's not the first time that's happened. It's a good sign. It means she's hydrated."

I authorized treatment for both pups who were

admitted to the hospital with the names of "X" for the black pup and "Y" for the beige one. Fear of their death prevented me from providing a name. At that point, I did not want to be emotionally attached.

"Will you put them up for a couple of weeks?" I asked. "I have to go to the U.S. in the morning to take

care of personal business."

"No problem. I'll take good care of them. I'll do what I can. Don't you worry. Have a safe trip."

"I'll give you a call in a few days, while I'm a way, to see how they're doing."

I drove home shouldering a ton of heartache.

Along the way, I thought about the missing third puppy and decided to see if it had returned.

Stopping at the former home of the puppies, I saw the neighbors who lived across the road. I walked to their front gate where they greeted me with smiles, handshakes, and then asked about the puppies.

"The beige one is very sick," I said. "I'm not sure she's going to make it."

"Sorry to hear that," a wrinkled old lady said, making the sign of the cross.

"On the other hand, the black pup seems to be doing well," I said. "She's eating, drinking, and running all over the place."

"That's wonderful," another neighbor said, removing his hat to wipe his brow. "Let's hope the beige one survives."

"Thank you. I hope so too. I'm pulling for her."

At that moment, I felt a welling up of profound sadness. My eyes burned. I feared I would cry, but I managed to hold back my tears. I swallowed hard, cleared my throat, and then asked, "Have any of you seen the second black puppy?"

An elderly, frail looking woman, swinging

upright in her porch hammock next door. called, "I spend a lot of time out here; I see everything that goes on this street. I didn't see any more dogs or the black puppy."

"That's not what I wanted to hear," I said. "I'm going to look around the house. See if the puppy might have returned, maybe sicker than before, or with an injury."

The neighbors pondered my idea then volunteered to help me search.

On "all fours," we searched under and around the building and nearby bushes but to no avail. I felt frustrated and dejected. I wanted to believe the puppy was happy, healthy, and safe on the lap of a loving, adoptive forever owner.

Back in America, the beige puppy's welfare weighed heavy on my mind. After a few days, I tried several times to phone the vet to inquire about the dogs' health. Each attempt met a different failure to connect.

Unable to contact the vet, I decided to call a friend who lived near my beach house. After several attempts, I was able to reach her. I explained the situation and asked her to visit the hospital then let me know about the puppy's health. She said she would and agreed to call me back.

Most villages in Mexico have no land-line phones. Villagers use prepaid cell phones, usually purchasing talk time in increments of $0.20 (US). No prepaid phone time meant no calling.

After several days without hearing from my friend, I tried to call her. I couldn't make contact, so I presumed she had no prepaid time. Encountering failure after failure to contact the vet or my friend, I gave up trying. I felt frustrated by my inability to get information about the pups. I reconciled myself to waiting until I returned to Mexico to learn their fate.

The fateful day arrived. I returned to Mexico and then hurried to the Puppy Palace, where to my surprise, I found it closed.

Strange, I thought. *The clinic is usually open in the afternoon.*

After knocking several times on the clinic door, a neighbor peeked from her half-opened door to investigate the noise. I told the woman my name and why I was knocking on the clinic door.

The woman said, "The vet . . . she had to make an emergency house call—to see a sick dog." Looking at her watch, she said, "Doc's been gone about an hour. She'll be back soon."

"Thanks, I'll wait," I said, feeling anxious.

I took a seat in one of the plastic chairs in the vet's outdoor reception area and waited. It seemed I waited a month as my anxiety mounted. I wanted to know how my dogs were doing. After all, they were just beyond the locked door behind me.

Fifteen minutes later, and many games of solitaire on my cell phone, the doctor arrived. *Hallelujah!*

"Hello," she said, putting her bag on the porch and giving me a hug and a continental kiss. "Welcome back. How was your flight? Everything okay in the US?"

"Everything went well—except for my inability to contact you. I don't know why, but for two weeks, I couldn't get a call through to anyone in Mexico. What's going on with the phone service?"

"The phone company has had problems with their cell towers. That's why you had problems. As a matter of fact, the towers still aren't working as they should."

Before the vet reminded me of which country I was in, I blurted, "I know. I'm in Mexico—not the

United States. Things are different here."

She laughed then said, "You can say that again. Sometimes, I wonder why I stay here."

I wondered if all this chit chat was a way to avoid talking about my dogs. With shakiness in my voice, I asked about the health of the puppies. The vet was silent and stone faced as she opened several locks on the clinic door.

"Come in," she said, placing her keys on a table whose legs were covered with gnaw marks made by one or more wood-hungry dogs.

She walked behind her paper-strewn desk then sat down in a swiveling, executive-style leather chair. It squeaked as she turned toward me.

"Come, sit beside the desk," she said, gesturing toward a side chair.

The squeak of her chair broke the silence as she turned toward the desk's work area. First, she templed her fingers in front of her chest and then placed her hands on the desk top. In a detached, professional tone, she told me about the black puppy. She shuffled through the puppy's medical records as she spoke in great detail about the black pup's slow but steady improvement.

"She had several anti-mange baths and slowly regrew hair in the inflamed and bare areas," the vet said, turning to another page of the record. "The anti-parasitic medication created the expected amount of diarrhea . . . She took milk and water from day one. Soon afterwards, we started small amounts of solid foods, without any problems. Her bloated abdomen has returned to near-normal size and should continue to shrink over the coming weeks as her nutrition improves."

Pausing to look at a different page of the black dog's medical record, she continued, "The pup has gained two pounds and is ready for discharge." She looked up from the record and smiled. "You should return the puppy in four weeks for follow up care and one more vaccination."

Closing the medical record, the vet handed me a four by six-inch brochure whose blue cover contained the clinic's name, address and phone number along with space for a dog's name.

"This is your black dog's medical record," the vet said. "You, or the dog's owner, should keep it. There's a space for dates of vaccinations, medications, etc. Bring this record with you each time you bring the dog in for care."

All of a sudden, I realized that I hadn't given much thought about what I would do with two puppies. After all, I already had Chico.

After a pause in conversation, I mustered the courage to ask, "How's the beige puppy doing?"

A pause ensued then the doctor said, "I'm sorry, but . . . I have bad news."

The vet had not said the word *dead,* but why should she? I detected the unspoken word in the tone of her voice. I slumped back in my chair. "What happened?"

Taking time to choose her words, the vet said, "The beige puppy continuously refused milk and water. We tried to force feed her with a syringe as I told you we would, but she resisted our efforts. I became so worried about her that I took her home where I tried day and night to force feed her, but she refused to take anything."

I didn't want to hear the remainder of the pup's medical history, but I forced myself to listen as my heart broke.

The doctor continued, "Over a few days, the pup went to sleep and couldn't be aroused. Her respirations became more and more shallow—then labored and then . . . they ceased." The doctor's words trailed off as she said, "She died peacefully from renal failure."

Suddenly, a landslide of sorrow crashed onto my psyche. Despite my efforts not to, I cried.

The vet came from behind her desk to comfort me. She pulled my head against her body. The smell of dog cologne from her skirt filled my nostrils as I wept for the loss of a puppy that had been in my life for less than a month.

After a minute or so, I regained my composure.

"What did you do with her?" I asked.

In America, dead animals are often cremated. In Mexico almost never.

"I buried her in my backyard," the vet said. "Would you like to visit the grave?"

I pondered the question for a moment then said, "Yes." I dreaded the trip, but I had to go. I needed closure.

"Okay, I'll drive. It's only twenty minutes away."

The vet's car had been sitting in the hot sun; its interior and seat covers were almost too hot to sit on. The vet lowered our windows, started the engine, and then the air conditioner.

We rode in silence. The drive gave me time to emotionally absorb the loss of the puppy. I couldn't shake the image of her small, comfort-seeking brown eyes staring from her scrawny little head. I remembered the feeble and shaky gait that barely moved her frail body; the labored breathing associated with her every effort; the tucked tail-of-fear she presented at every effort to help her.

Had I brought more fear and discomfort into her life than I had eliminated? Would she have been better off if I had left her where I discovered her?

The thoughts troubled me even though I knew there was no right answer. Nevertheless, I couldn't push the disturbing thoughts from my mind.

I was happy the vet remained quiet as she drove. My emotions were too near the surface and had me so shaken I couldn't think clearly, much less talk.

We soon reached the vet's home. We walked along a flower-bordered path that paralleled the length of her home. It led to a large backyard. She had one of the few lawns in Progreso. Because grass needed constant watering, most people didn't bother with the expense or effort required to maintain grass.

Festooned with flowering tropical plants, the yard looked more like the Garden of Eden than a Progreso lawn. The sweet fragrance of flowers flooded the area like incense at high mass. Among the plants grew a beautiful bougainvillea that draped itself over the back and side walls. Its boughs bore a profusion of purple blossoms. The flower-laden limbs seemed to "tumble" toward the spot where I knew we were headed.

For a moment, I stood in the middle of the lawn and thought of the yard as a beautiful cemetery where a warm breeze ferried the songs of a neighbor's parakeets.

Fifty feet ahead, my gaze fell upon a breach in the green of the lawn. I saw a small mound of brown soil that had been recently worked. Words were not necessary to tell me that spot marked the grave. I didn't want to believe this small grave held such a precious treasure, but it did.

My leaden feet carried me reluctantly toward the mound until I stood where I didn't want to be. I made the sign of the cross and cried then sobbed. I could hardly breathe.

The vet put her arm around my shoulder then hugged me. "That's okay," she said. "I'm so sorry. I wished there was more we could have done."

After a minute, I took, from my pocket, one of two bone-shaped dog treats I had taken to the clinic in anticipation of giving one to each of my puppies. I knelt beside the grave then pushed one end of the treat into the loose soil. The treat became a small tombstone.

This isn't the way I imagined I'd be giving you your first treat, I said to myself.

I realized that I had accepted total ownership of the puppy, but I had hoped for a different kind of reunion—a tail wagging, face licking one. My heart ached, knowing my treat would never be enjoyed.

Taking a minute or two to regain my inner strength, I said, "I'm ready to leave."

"Are you sure you don't want to stay longer?" the vet asked, rubbing my shoulder. "You could sit here in the shade, and I could make some lemonade."

"Thanks, but I'm ready to go.

The vet drove us back to the clinic.

"I'll be back in the morning to get the black puppy," I muttered. My words were almost inaudible and filled with a sense of loss.

"That's fine," she said. "However, if you want to visit the black pup today that would be okay."

"No, thanks. I couldn't. Not now."

My original plan had been to get medical care for the three puppies and then return them to the house where I had found them. Now, however, only one pup remained, and I didn't feel comfortable leaving the fifteen-week old pup to roam alone where I had found her. I imagined all kinds of mishaps that might befall a puppy given her old environment. I doubted I could find her a forever home and felt somewhat stuck with another dog, but perhaps, I wanted to be.

The next morning, I purchased a doghouse and

all the necessary accessories. I then drove to the clinic and claimed my puppy. I placed her on the front passenger seat. Her heft allowed her to hold her footing and not be thrown from the seat by jolts or bumps along the way, however, her demeanor suggested some uneasiness about the ride. She jumped with fright at every bang, boom, clang or jolt, so I placed her in my lap, but all she wanted to do was play "ostrich." She pushed her head into my right armpit in search of security.

I let her "hide" while I stroked her back, trying to calm her. Her recently bathed coat glistened in the sunlight and felt like silk. The vet had sprayed her with the now familiar cologne used to cover a dog's normal canine odor.

During the drive, I realized I had named this puppy, "Y" for the hospital record, but "Y" is not a proper name for a dog.

I've got to come up with something better than "Y." I'll call her Blackie . . . nah . . . too obvious. I considered Spot, since she had a small white spot on her chin. *Nah. Spot is too obvious. I already have a Chico. Why not a Chica?*

That was it, I'd call my newest family member, Chica.

Now I had a Chico and a Chica.

At the beach house, Chica was anxious to leave the car before it stopped. When I opened my door, her large paws scampered over my thighs, descended onto the door threshold, and then onto the sand where she began to run around the compound as if she remembered being there three weeks earlier. She sniffed everything in sight. I wanted to believe she searched for the scent of her dead sister, but Chica searched for a place to pee. After finding the spot where she had peed weeks earlier, she relieved herself.

My caretaker, Hugo, his wife, and year-old son came out to see the newest family addition. Chica wagged her tail and jumped with excitement as the trio arrived.

Hugo's son, Juan, was fascinated by the dog's activities. Juan pointed toward the dog and babbled. Waddling, he and Chica approached each other at eye level. As Chica's nose came within six inches of Juan's face, she licked it twice. He laughed then cried. Chica's floppy ears shot straight up as she turned and ran from the wailing boy.

Over the next several days, Chica seemed attached to my heel. I couldn't take a step for fear of stepping on her large paws. I could tell from their size she would be a large dog, and indeed, over time, she took on the characteristics of a large Labrador Retriever.

Each day brought her visible growth as well as a limitless appetite. No matter how full her food bowl, she ate every morsel.

As her appetite increased so did the piles of poop that had to be removed from the "sandbox" yard.

I noticed her water bowl needed to be frequently refilled. My concerns turned to thoughts of a possible pituitary or brain tumor, diabetes, or a bladder infection as the cause of her constant thirst. I monitored her water intake for a few days and then phoned the vet.

"Chica has been drinking a lot of water," I said.

"Between three or four liters a day and I'm concerned something is wrong."

"That's a lot of water for a dog her size. Bring her in, and I'll examine her."

The next morning, Chica and I set out for the Puppy Palace.

The vet used a special "dipstick" to screen for a urinary infection and increased urine sugar.

"Good news," the doctor said, feeling the dog's abdomen. "These simple tests are normal, but to check for pituitary problems, we would have to send a blood sample to Mexico City. That would be very expensive and time consuming. Since Chica appears to be doing well, I suggest we just monitor her for a while."

"How much longer?" I asked.

"Oh, another two weeks provided she continues to do well."

"Okay. I'll keep an eye on her and report back in two weeks."

After two weeks, Chica's water consumption returned to normal, so the vet and I decided not to pursue other tests.

While Chica's love proved to be consistent, her bathroom habits weren't. For a day or two, she would use the "sandbox," which was always at-the-ready, and then for some unknown reason, she would make a concrete surface her toilet.

The caretaker and I were tired of cleaning up her messes, so we decided to chain her in the front yard after each feeding. We kept her there until she had answered the call of nature. Having done so, she was allowed to roam off the chain, but I did not allow her access to water or food while unchained.

After a week of training and no "mistakes," Chica appeared to be a reformed girl.

Since she and Chico were beach dogs, they were always carriers of varying amounts of sand. For this reason, they weren't allowed in the house. Therefore, I didn't worry about "house-breaking" either of them.

My dogs became close companions for each other. Where you saw one, you saw the other.

Chico, older and larger, reveled in playing with Chica who would mercilessly chew his stubby tail. Their interactions led me to believe Chico wanted to prepare her for the tough life of a Yucatecan beach dog. She would soon have to defend herself from stray beach dogs, and Chico seemed hell-bent on providing the appropriate self-defense training. He had taken on the role of mother dog, the parent most often responsible for providing defensive training.

There were all kinds of play fights between the two dogs, but every once in a while, one or the other would bite too hard. There would be a yelp, a short pause in play, and then the heated activities resumed. I sometimes wondered if one of their games might be called "swallow the dog," since each often tried to engulf the other's head in its mouth.

I often felt sorry for Chico when he appeared to have had enough rough-housing play but couldn't escape the more playful Chica. On those occasions, I chained her until Chico could rest. Having rested, he would carry a toy in his mouth and teasingly offer it to her. Just as she came within snatching distance of the toy, Chico ran away, the bauble dangling from his mouth. Chica always gave chase.

Most mornings, I'd be awakened by their playful growling under my window. By evening, they were so exhausted they observed a respectful bedtime hour and remained quiet all night. I delighted that they related so well, and I appreciated their respect that allowed me a peaceful night's sleep.

April arrived, and Chica continued to grow. At about five to seven months of age, she stood shoulder-to-shoulder with Chico. At that age, I needed to have her spayed. I did not want her contributing to the canine population. I, nor the village, needed any more dogs. Secondly, the spaying would reduce her chance of developing breast cancer.

I discussed the issue with the vet who decided the operation should occur in May. I needed to return to the United States in mid-April, but I would return to Mexico in May for the surgery. I planned to stay for a week after Chica's surgery. I wanted that time to make sure she did well because when I left I would not return to Mexico until mid-November.

In late May, I returned to Mexico and could not wait to see the dogs.

A beautiful sunset filled the sky with blazing shades of red and orange as I arrived at the beach. I pressed a button and waited for the garage door to move aside.

As I drove into the open ended parking space, an automatic light sensor turned on my car's headlights. The dogs ran into the headlight's beam where they acted like a chorus line of untrained dancers under a spotlight. They jumped about and wagged their tails, like a cheap circus act.

As I exited the car, Chica ran to my opened door and extended her head to be patted. Chico soon joined her. The three of us had a joyful reunion with hugs and licks that seemed to go on forever.

It's nice to be back, I thought.

Over the next three days, the dogs and I got reacquainted. We took early-morning walks on the beach to drain their excess energy, so I would have peace and quiet later in the day.

During this period, I monitored Chica to assure myself she was healthy enough to undergo surgery.

The day of surgery, I drove to the vet's office. When we arrived, I placed a restraining collar around Chica's neck then coaxed her from the car. She paused a few times to sniff other dogs' markings.

In the clinic waiting area, she sat at my feet,

waiting for the vet. From her seated position, she sniffed the floor and then the leg of the chair in which I sat. She wanted to explore more of the waiting area, but a simple tug on the leash brought her back to the spot I had chosen for her to wait.

In a short while, the vet entered. Looking at me while extending a hand of greeting toward Chica, the vet said, "Good morning. How are things going?"

"We're doing well," I said, tugging at Chica's leash.

"Let's take her to the exam room, so I can get a look at her."

The vet reached for the leash. Chica licked his out-stretched hand. To Chica's delight, the vet scratched and then patted her head.

"I'm glad she doesn't bite the hand that cures her," the vet chuckled.

"How's everything going for her?" the vet asked.

"Great as far as I can tell."

"Would you mind putting her on the table?" the doctor asked.

"Okay. Chica, up we go."

With a heave, I lifted her onto the stainless steel table where her preoperative exam began.

"Everything seems to be in order," the doctor said, scratching behind Chica's ears. "She should do well. I've planned surgery for two o'clock."

The vet pushed a button on his desk. Seconds later, an assistant entered the room. "Will you take Chica to cage one?" he said. "She's to be spayed this afternoon."

Looking at me, he said, "If you want, you may follow Chica to the holding area and see that she's comfortably settled in."

I accepted the invitation.

The assistant opened the cage door then invited Chica to enter. At first, she hesitated then looked back at me questioningly.

I took the leash, gave it a slight tug, and said, "Go to bed."

Chica lived among Mexicans, so I wasn't sure how much English she understood, but she moved into the cage without hesitation.

Thankfully, she's not too anxious.

I poked my finger through the space between the thin bars of the cage then rubbed her snout. I felt comfortable about her apparent state of mental health and left, looking over my shoulder several times to make eye contact and offer assurance. She stared at me but made not a sound.

At home, I began the surgical vigil. At 4:00 p.m., the vet phoned me.

"How did everything go?" I asked.

"She did well. Surgery was easy. I found nothing unusual."

Chuckling, I asked, "You didn't perforate the bowel did you?"

"Hell no! I'm a better surgeon than that. Chica is in her cage and wide awake. We'll wait six hours before we give her water, but she should be ready to eat by tomorrow."

I felt relieved. "Could I visit her around 10:00 a.m.?" I asked.

"That's fine. See you then."

The clinic didn't open until noon, but the vet made an exception for me. He greeted me at the door.

"Buenos dias," I said. "How's she doing?"

"Come back to the holding area," the vet said, holding the door open. "See for yourself."

The vet led the way to the holding area where I saw Chica in her cage. She recognized me, wagged her tail, and started to stand, the vet extended his hand to prevent her from doing so.

"I used absorbable sutures to close her incision," the vet said, "They aren't as strong as silk, but they'll save you a clinic visit to have them removed. Don't worry. They'll be absorbed over time. However, too much activity could put a strain on the incision. Could cause it to open so keep her physically quiet."

"Has she eaten yet?" I asked.

"So far, she has taken small amounts of water," the vet said, looking at his watch, "but it's time for her to have some solid food. Would you like to feed her?"

"Absolutely."

The vet's assistant placed some dry pellets in my hand, and then I offered one to Chica. She quickly gobbled it up. I offered a few more. She gobbled them up as if she was starved.

"She must be very hungry," I said.

"That's enough," the vet said. "She shouldn't have any more for several hours. I want to be sure her bowel has regained enough activity to handle more solids."

I wanted to feed her more, but I knew she should wait a while before having more food. I substituted gentle head strokes, along with hugs, instead of the food she wanted.

After a few minutes of one-on-one time, I hugged her, then petted her through the cage, and then locked its door.

"Thanks for doing such a great job, Doctor. I'll visit again tomorrow."

The vet nodded. "She'll be ready for home then."

"If you don't mind, I'd like to leave her here for forty-eight hours. I have some concerns about taking her tomorrow because of the sutures *and* her very playful brother. I want to be sure there won't be any complications due to Chico's rough housing—like

85

having Chica's belly burst open."

"No problem," the vet said. "She can stay for a few more days."

Over the next three days, Chica ate and drank normally and visited with an older, sedentary dog owned by the veterinarian.

On the third post op day, I took Chica home. She didn't mind the car ride. This time, she planted her front paws on the window ledge to peer at the country side. On several occasions, I stopped her from stretching her torso for fear of putting a strain on her stitches. Soon, she seemed content to sit on the seat in exchange for my rubbing her head.

At home, I turned off the car ignition then open-ed my door. Suddenly, a black blur darted across my body, past my out-stretched hands, and then out the door and onto the sand where Chica let out a yelp.

I cringed in fear. Expecting the worse, I closed my eyes. I didn't want to see that her bowels had spilled onto the sand.

For a second, I held my breath then forced myself to assess the damage. "Oh my God," I yelled. The sand was not covered with blood and guts.

I felt a flood of relief wash over me. She hadn't disemboweled herself but played with Chico as though nothing had happened.

During the week, Chica and Chico resumed rough house playing—much to my dismay. I tried to keep Chica from hyperextending her body, for fear she would disrupt the incision, but holding her back became an impossible task.

With my physical interference, dog play would stop for a few minutes but then resume. I drove my-self crazy pursuing the impossible goal of limiting her physical activities. I had no choice but to relent or keep one of the dogs caged—something I did not want to do for fear of making matters worse. Then it dawned on me, *IF* anything bad should happen, it should happen in my presence so prompt attention could be given to the situation. Much to my joy, nothing bad happened.

The first week of June arrived and that meant the days were hot and humid—time to return to the States where a cooler summer awaited.

I said my goodbyes to Hugo and his wife, Maria. I reminded them I would not return until November.

"Don't forget the dogs are to be fed twice a day," I told Hugo, "and please make sure their water bowls are always full. It's going to be a hot summer, and the dogs will need lots of water."

Chica slept in her doghouse, and Chico barked at children playing on the beach. When I called, the dogs came running, tails wagging. I rubbed and hugged them then gave each a doggie treat.

I found it hard to say goodbye to them.

I opened the garage door then backed onto the sand road. I was careful not to run over the dogs as they walked near the front wheels, wagging their tails.

Hugo and his wife waved goodbye.

I pulled away from the house. In the rearview mirror, I watched as the dogs followed me along the road. With a lump in my throat, I sped up leaving them a half block from the house where they gave up pursuit. They sat on their haunches like sentinels at a Chinese temple. Shoulder-to-shoulder, they stared at my departing car.

Looking over my shoulder, I could see the two of them keeping guard on the road that would someday bring me back.

#

Americans are known for personifying their pets.

For many people, pets become surrogate children.

It has been said intelligent dogs have the intellect of a three or four-year-old child, and that dogs live in the moment, holding no grudges.

Who knows how accurate these "old wives' tales" are, but I hoped my dogs would not think they had been abandoned—again—and hoped they knew they were loved.

Every once in a while, when I can muster the courage, I take out the photos of Chica and her beige sister. The pictures were taken just minutes after the pups were rescued.

I look at Beige's picture and see her frail body, spindly legs, sad eyes, and tucked tail. I marvel at how she struggled so valiantly to live.

I hope there is a puppy heaven. A heaven where every puppy receives a set of angel's wings.

"It doesn't matter if an animal can reason. It matters only that it is capable of suffering, and that is why I consider it my neighbor."

Albert Schweitzer

Chapter 4

Gloria

A blanket of clouds shadowed Yucatan's scrub jungle, concealing creeping, crawling things small, large, and ominous. Some evoke fear and some prompt pity. My face-to-face encounter with horror began in these shadows and haunts me to this day.

Travelling west from Progreso, along the northern coast of Yucatan, one passes several villages. Yucalpaten, population 1,200, is home to a naval base. West of Yucalpaten is Chelem, a gritty fishing village, population 7,000. In the past, most of its inhabitants worked as fishermen, an industry now in decline—due to overfishing. Waiting along village beaches are overturned fishing boats in need of a coat of paint and a resurgence of commercial fishing.

A single paved highway traverses the coast of the Yucatan Peninsula delineating the north side of Chelem's town square known as the *zocalo*. All who use this road quickly become familiar with this landmark. The plaza supports: vendors, fiestas, outdoor restaurants, and *tiendas* (small stores), selling ice, brooms, packaged foods, water, colas, household staples, and carnivals that visit the village several times a year.

Teenagers and adults congregate on the square Saturday nights to cuddle, gossip, and drink Coca Cola until the wee hours of the morning.

Vendors, selling cheap clothing from trucks in the evenings, crowd the streets. Shoppers strain their eyes to examine the merchandise illuminated by gas lanterns.

Flatbed trucks, loaded with boxes of cheap, Mexican-made shoes often set up shop there. The shoe vendors attract buyers by blasting the night with poor quality recordings of, off-key, mariachi bands booming from VW Beetle size "boom boxes" and providing free samples of homemade salsa.

The so-called music can compress your chest as subsonic-bass notes erupt like volcanic explosions, shaking the boom boxes that contain several thirty inch speakers.

The evening air is often filled with the aroma of pork being blackened on homemade grills, made from oil drums, parked at the edge of the plaza.

The din of the evening's activity is often punctuated by the sound of shattering glass as someone, who has had one too many beers, loses their grip on a bottle, and it crashes to the pavement.

Stray dogs roam about in search of food scraps or something to drink. For the most part, the dogs are ignored and scamper aside as pedestrians or cars pass by.

Life is simple here, and smiles are seen everywhere. The villagers' harsh life is filled with happiness for what they have. They don't fret over what they don't have.

The ever present *topez,* or speed bump, located

on all sides of the town square, insures cars move slowly. Drivers, not wearing seat belts, drive slowly to avoid being catapulted from their seats. This passive method of enforcing the speed limit provides an opportunity for drivers to survey the local square, its buildings, inhabitants, and roaming animals. One can see horses, cats, donkeys, cows, chickens, and feral dogs roaming about.

Older women, with wizened and leathery faces etched by the sun, are seen everywhere, wearing traditional attire, which are long, white cotton dresses decorated with wide bands of colorful machine-embroidered flowers at the shoulders and around the hem. The traditional hand-embroidered version is time consuming and expensive. However, wealthy brides often choose to wear a silk wedding gown decorated with these traditional hand-embroidered flowers—often made with off-white thread.

White, pink, red, salmon, or purple bougainvillea boughs tumble over stucco walls, separating small, brightly-colored concrete-block homes. Visitors always comment on these colorful sites where village life moves at its own pedestrian pace.

One day, I slowed my car to three miles an hour to avoid bouncing over a *topez* near Chelem's *zocalo*. The slow speed allowed me time to enjoy a beautiful, thirty-foot-tall, flowering tree on my left. I had seen the tree before, but it had strange and sparse foliage on its twiggy limbs earlier. Now in late winter, the tree blazed with vivid, red-orange fluffy blossoms that dazzled me with their beauty.

It wasn't this beautiful when I last passed this way, I thought.

I stopped my car in the middle of the road to admire the incredible sight. *I have to come back and photograph this before the blossoms are gone.*

Driving away, I looked at the ground beneath the tree. A slight breeze had rustled the tree's leaves and blossoms, permitting a few rays of sunlight to reach the ground. Sun-speckled shadows danced over fallen blossoms scattered on the sandy soil as if strewn for a bride's walk down the aisle. There in the shadows, I noticed something. At first, I thought I had seen a clump of old rags someone had tossed aside. However, the "rags" moved.

Did the wind just blow those rags about? No . . . that's not a rag.

I stared at the unknown object. Behind me, an impatient driver honked his horn. I waved to indicate he should pass as I stared into the dancing shadows beneath the tree. This time, I could make out the outline of a dog's head. It appeared to be a blood-hound, the kind I often saw in my home state of Tennessee. Its long, floppy ears helped to outline drooping jowls that fell from a wide, black-tipped snout. The dog's dark eyes almost disappeared under its drooping upper eyelids. The sagging lower lids revealed a bright red coloration of the part of the eye that is normally white. The face looked tired, thin, and haggard.

I whistled at the dog, hoping it would approach and accept some dog treats I held out the window at arm's length. Instead, the animal tilted its head toward me, its blood colored eyes staring in my direction, but the dog remained in its prone position. Except for its momentary glance, the dog ignored me.

The dog and a small cinder-block house shared the shade of this broad, flowering tree. In front of the house sat two older women. Their cheap, white-plastic chairs, ubiquitous in the Yucatan, strained to support the women's weight. The women stared at me curiously. I backed my car fifty feet then pulled to their side of the road. At one mile an hour, I drove to within eight feet of the dog's resting place.

Please don't run away doggy.

I had learned not to throw treats to feral dogs, for despite their hunger, many of them perceived thrown treats as a threat, causing the animal to flee. Their retreat often left the food for a healthier dog instead of the one that needed it.

As the hound looked on, I dropped five treats on the ground where they scattered twelve inches from my car. After contemplating me, the car, and the treats, the dog wobbled toward the food. As it approached the nearest treat, the older woman walked toward the dog. The dog cowered.

The woman bent down, dragging her long, rose-colored, embroidered dress in the sand and picked up one of the bone-shaped treats. She smelled it, broke and examined it, shrugged, turned toward her companion, and said something. The seated woman nodded. The examiner turned toward me, smiled, and then dropped the treat near the dog.

Does she think I'm trying to poison the dog? I wonder if it's her's?

The inquisitive woman returned to her chair, and the dog reapproached the treats. This provided me an opportunity to evaluate her health. From her neck hung a contrived "collar" and "leash" made from a long piece of brown lamp cord. An intact electrical plug, at the loose end of the cord, dragged behind her.

I could tell the hound had once been a mother by the teats that hung from her belly. She looked wasted. Her skin sagged and her ribs stood out like the spines of an accordion's bellows.

As she munched a treat, I noted several other things about her body that caused me concern. High on the left hip was a skin ulcer measuring four inches in diameter. Its irregular shape and raised edges suggested it was a chronic ulcer. A reddish crust in its center suggested fresh bleeding.

The appearance of the sore made me want to look away. However, upon further inspection, I saw she had no hair. Unlike other dogs in the area rendered hairless by mange, this dog did not have the overall inflamed skin one associated with mange. The dog's skin was dark brown.

I wondered if the brown color camouflaged the usual signs of mange. Surprisingly, the dog didn't have the bloated belly of starvation seen in so many feral dogs.

I delighted in watching the dog eat the treats, for I knew villagers would not feed her. It was that neglect that caused me to carry dog treats in my car.

Using my rearview mirror, I watched the dog eat the last of the treats as I drove away. I confess; I had a sense of pride knowing I had helped her.

The image of the dog in my mirror grew smaller and smaller. However, when I saw her limp across the road and head down a side street, I stopped the car. I decided to follow her to see if she might be going to her home. I made a "U" turn in the middle of the road and headed to the street where she had disappeared from view.

I slowed my car to a crawl and followed her. Looking weary, she hugged a whitewashed wall that helped delineated the width of the sand-road. Barking dogs on the opposite side of the road did not deter her. She trudged along determined to pursue her goal.

Half-a-block ahead, I saw the dog's objective—a puddle of water at the edge of the road. The water had the appearance of left over carwash water. Whitish foam covered its surface. She sniffed the water, and after a moment's hesitation, her tongue entered the foamy liquid. She lapped at it until her thirst, or taste limits, stopped her drinking. Sated, she turned from the pool and walked into the shade of a nearby palm tree that provided a cool resting place.

I left her in peace, wondering where she would go for her next drink once the remaining water had drained into the thirsty sand.

Hours later, on my return trip through Chelem, I passed the area where I had first seen the starving dog. She wasn't there. Nevertheless, I scatter a few treats, where I had seen her, presuming she would return. If she did, supper awaited, however, I hoped she would return before other animals found the food.

Several days later, I drove past the tree where the beautiful blossoms persisted. I slowed to admire their beauty and to look for the starving dog. Sure enough, she rested there, on her belly, in her usual spot. With her head held high and her right paw draped over her left one, she appeared almost regal, even haughty.

That pose . . . Her pose reminded me of someone famous but whom? I laughed aloud as I recalled the name of the "someone." It was Gloria Swanson.

Ms. Swanson, a silent film movie star, had to utilize body-language skills to convey emotions. Somehow, this dog impressed me as doing the same thing.

Despite her health problems, the dog never barked or whined. She acted as if she was healthy, but she was not.

With the image of Gloria Swanson locked in my mind, I noticed what I thought was a long narrow area of sunlight on the back of the dog's neck.

Maybe Gloria is wearing a necklace, I told myself and then chuckled. *Hmmm. Is that . . . sunlight or not?*

"Oh my god." I jerked my head backwards in horror. I closed my eyes for a moment then refocused them on the dog's neck. The old electrical cord was missing and had been replaced with a clearly delineated gash across the back of her neck. The edges of the "incision" were so sharp they could have been inflicted by a surgeon's scalpel. The incision appeared to be twelve inches long, extending around the back and both sides of her neck. If the cut had been much longer, it would have encircled her neck.

Hound dogs have loose skin, not only because of the breed, but in the case of this dog, weight loss played a role. Starvation was presumed to be the culprit. The latter exaggerated the skin's looseness.

The cut gapped to a width of about two and a half inches when she lowered her head. I winced at the sight of this fresh, bloodless wound.

The deepest layer of the skin, lying directly over her neck muscles, glistened with a silvery-white color in the sunlight. Through this thin layer of tissue, I could see her neck muscles contract and then relax as she moved her head from side-to-side.

"Oh, my god, what happened to you?" Even though I was alone, I had a conversation with myself about the dog's condition. "That wound has to be intentional, but why would a monster of a person have done such a hideous thing to a poor defenseless dog?"

For a moment, I thought the electrical cord leash / collar might have caused the injury but how? The collar portion of the electrical cord had not fitted tightly nor did it have sharp edges.

I sat motionless for a moment, pondering the situation and observing the horrible sight.

God. What should I do?

Catching her would be difficult, and the nearest vet was miles away. The only thing I could think of was to offer her food. I dropped some treats on the ground and waited for her response. For a while, nothing happened. I began to think she might be in so much pain she would not move—even for food.

Emotionally shaken, I prepared to drive away, but the dog rose and made her way to the treats her gait plodding and determined. She stood motionless with her head over the first treat. After a few seconds, she lowered her head to eat.

I almost vomited as I watched the unfettered skin on the back of her neck slide forward as she dropped her head. The skin slid so much, I thought the cut edge would fall over her eyes. Yet, she uttered not a sound. I couldn't bear to watch her sliced skin's movement.

Heartsick, I drove toward home too shocked and fearful to watch her in the rearview mirror.

At home, my healthy rescue-dogs jumped with joy at seeing me. I hugged them to my chest and tolerated their many licks as the memory of the horrifying sight I had just experienced seared itself in my memory.

On shopping day, I drove to Progreso, knowing I had to pass the tree where I had seen Gloria. As I approached the spot, I told myself, I won't look under the tree. I'll drive past it like nothing has happened. I will ignore everything around me.

Frank, you know you can't not look. You're going to look. You know you'll look.

Not trusting myself to ignore the dog, I turned off the main road two blocks before I reached the dog's resting spot. I drove two blocks south of the main road and then far enough east to pass the maimed dog. A bit unhappy with myself, I loosened my grip on the steering wheel and breathed a sigh of relief. I had avoided the avoidable.

I finished shopping then headed home. Normally, I would have traveled through Chelem, past the town square and then the street where Gloria rested. That day, I mentally mapped a route of avoidance.

As I approached Chelem, I encountered a number of orange traffic-control cones placed across the road. A part time policeman I knew directed traffic.

I stopped beside him and asked, "Pedro, what's happening?"

Pedro leaned a forearm on my window sill while waving traffic around me. He smiled then said, "A carnival is setting up in the square. Traffic has to be diverted to avoid the activities. Move forward and follow the instructions of the officer ahead. See ya."

Traffic moved like a sloth. The passable roadway narrowed because a number of locals had double-parked, making it difficult for drivers to negotiate a path.

I moved like a snail through the maze of parked cars, trucks, wagons, and adult-sized three-wheeled bicycles used by locals for transport activities. Traffic stopped for a moment as an officer permitted a horse-drawn wagon to cross the road. The officer blew his whistle and motioned for me to proceed.

I drove along the western side of the plaza, heading south. At its southern corner, another officer directed traffic to turn right. The beautiful flowering tree loomed a block away.

"Oh, no," I said. "I'll have to pass Gloria's spot." *I'm not going to look. I'll stare straight ahead . . . ignore everything around me. I don't want to see her again.*

Traffic moved an inch at a time. The cars ahead were, one-by-one, bouncing over a series of speed-bumps.

The afternoon sun was sinking and emblazoned my dirty windshield with a glare that blinded me. I turned on my windshield wipers then pushed the button to activate the washer, but there was no water. Between the windshield's coating of salt, from ocean breezes, sand, and the sun's glare, I had difficulty seeing the road. I slowed my car to lengthen the distance between me and the car ahead. I wanted to avoid an accident in case I had to stop suddenly.

An impatient driver behind me, sporting a horn larger than his vehicle, tooted his "pride" at my slow pace of driving. I ignored him and the cacophony of his plaything.

The chain of cars moved with the speed of a stone destined for a pyramid, but then, the space in front of my car widened, and I felt safer about driving into the glaring sunlight. It had been my intention to drive past the tree and the dog, if she was there, but how would I know? I wasn't going to look. I stared straight ahead.

So far, I haven't looked. I've succeeded. I can do it. I'm not going to look.

I breathed easier, for I knew I would escape the anxiety conjured by the sight of Gloria.

Three cars ahead, an old truck darted through a narrow opening in the string of slow moving cars. To avoid hitting the interloping vehicle, the lead car stopped abruptly. As in a chain reaction, we all slammed on our brakes. "Damn it!" I had stopped in the shadow of the beautiful tree. Its shadow eliminated the windshield glare that had obscured my line of sight. I had an unobstructed view of the ground under the tree.

I didn't want to look, but I couldn't help it. Unwillingly, maybe, I glanced to the right. Sure enough, Gloria was there, resting under the tree. Nothing had changed about her or her neck wound. I marveled that the wound did not appear infected. However, signs of rampant infection on her hip ulcer persisted.

How much can she endure?

I took a handful of dog-treats from the glove box,

opened the passenger-side window then tossed them on the shoulder of the road. Traffic cleared, and I pulled forward, feeling sorry for Gloria.

Over the following days, I couldn't shake my thoughts of her. I felt miserable about the hound's condition and decided I needed to share my misery with someone, so I called my veterinarian.

After discussing several care options, the doctor said, "I think it would be best if we put her 'down.'"

The decision caused me concern, but after additional reflection, my heart relented. I believed the dog lived a nightmare that would soon take her life. It would be better to die quietly than fend off rats trying to gnaw on her in her last hours of life.

The vet advised me she would be in Chelem on Thursday. We were to meet at 10:00 a.m. in the plaza. From there, we would locate the dog and do our business.

Punctuality is an obsession of mine. However, on the appointed morning, I took my time getting to the plaza. My car was filled with a troubling silence and disturbing thoughts of how our "business" would be best for the dog.

As I drove past the beautiful tree, I scanned its shade for the dog. I didn't see her. For a minute, I felt relieved.

I parked at the plaza at 9:55 a.m. Despite the, hour, the temperature had risen fast and the humidity levels were already at their zenith. I let the air conditioner run and lowered the sun visor to block the sun glare while I waited for the vet.

I craned my neck at every passing vehicle in an effort to ascertain whether or not the car was driven by her. At 10:15 a.m., the vet had not arrived. I decided to wait five minutes longer; if she hadn't arrived by then, I'd call her.

102

It's ten twenty, I thought, looking at my watch. *Maybe she can't get away.*

I dialed her number and waited as the ringing went on and on. She didn't answer.

What do I do now? She has never been late or intentionally incommunicado. Maybe she's out of phone time.

I decided to leave, so I could take care of some personal business. I felt relieved that the vet had not arrived. Somehow, killing out of love always bothered me. I wondered if putting Gloria down was the right thing to do?

I completed my errands then drove toward home. I passed the dog's resting place and scanned the shadows, but I didn't see her. Nevertheless, I dropped some treats. I wanted to believe she would return before another animal absconded with the food.

Over the following days, I passed Gloria's rest area numerous times. I didn't see her.

During one trip, I saw the lady who had examined the dog treats I had left weeks earlier. She sat motionless in her cheap, plastic chair, watching a man carry water bottles into a *tienda* across the street.

I have to talk to these ladies. See what they know about the old dog.

Heat and humidity hit me like a steamed towel as I left the comfort of my car to cross the sand-strewn pavement.

"*Buenos tardes, Señora,*" I said.

"*Tardes, Señor.*"

Pointing toward the shadows, I asked, "Have you seen the hound dog that used to shade herself there?"

"No, not for several days," an older-looking woman said, leaving the shade of the tree and walking toward me.

"Do you know how she got that horrible cut on

her neck?" I asked.

"No, but wasn't it awful?" the first lady asked. "Made me feel sorry for her."

"Do you know if she has an owner or is she a stray?"

"As far as I know, she's a stray," the women said in unison.

"If she comes back, would you give her these?" I asked, handing the ladies a bag of treats.

"Okay, *Señor*."

Three days later, I drove past the tree that still retained some blossoms and shading leaves. I looked for Gloria, but she was not there.

Driving east, out of town to go shopping, I scanned the plaza, the area around the Catholic Church, the fronts of a number of small restaurants, crossed the last *topez,* and then left the village. Gloria was nowhere to be seen.

I drove at a snail pace, de-stressing, and noting other flowering trees along the road. I slowed for a road gang removing trash from highway shoulders.

Further ahead, several men dug wild grasses growing along the pavement edge. I often wondered why locals removed something that helped prevent sand from blowing into their houses. One man raked the dislodged weeds into piles while another man supervised their burning.

A dog chased my car and nipped at my right-front tire. I stopped for a moment to see what the dog might do if he "caught" the tire. Once I stopped, the dog gave up the fight then mopped to the side of the road, stared at me, and then stretched out on the sand.

Three-hundred-fifty feet ahead, I saw an older man digging a hole on the left side of the road. He stopped digging, removed his hat, wiped his brow, and then resumed digging for a minute. After emptying the last spadesful of soil beside the road, he dropped the shovel.

I stopped my car in the middle of the highway, opposite the man, and watched as he picked up what looked like trash.

"Oh, my God!" I said, observing what I had thought was trash.

The man picked up Gloria. Gripping her rear legs, he held her emaciated body off the sand.

I gasped. "She's dead!"

Her right leg slipped from his grip, and her head hit the ground.

"Oh!" I yelled as if she had been harmed.

The man grabbed both rear legs and dragged her, like trash, toward the hole he had just dug. Her head bounced over the sand as she neared her final resting place.

Her eyes, filled with the stare of death, were partially covered by her long, floppy ears and the skin of her gaping neck wound. The man dropped her into the grave as if he had a piece of trash. Her right rear-leg failed to follow her body into the hole, so the grave digger kicked the protruding limb into the void.

"Oh no." I exited the car, and scampered toward the man. "What happened?" I asked—my voice breaking.

"Not sure," the man said, "I saw her lying here this morning while I was having a Coke on my porch. After some time, I noticed she hadn't moved, so I came to investigate. She was dead. Since she died on my property, I decided I'd bury her—before rot set in."

The old man removed his dirty, wide-brimmed straw hat and wiped sweat from his brow with what had once been a white handkerchief. He then moved his cigarette to the opposite side of his mouth and took a drag.

"Was she your dog?" he asked, wiping his hands on his pants as if trying to wipe off a piece of death.

"No, she wasn't anybody's dog, just everybody's. She was just another stray that somehow managed to endure people's neglect and abuse."

I shared my knowledge of the dog's life and thanked the man for his kindness in burying her.

"I know she wasn't your dog, but it seems you took a liking to her."

"It was more like pity, but I guess I did," I said, trying to maintain my composure.

I walked toward my car, but my conscience gnawed at me. *I can't leave things like this. I've got to go back.*

Turning, I asked, "*Señor*, would you mind if I finished your work?"

"No," he replied, holding out the shovel.

I stared into the shallow grave and grieved at the sight of the body that bore the marks of man's cruelty.

She's all crunched up in that little hole. She can't rest in peace like that.

I lengthened the hole six inches. I wanted Gloria to be stretched out—not crunched up. Even in death, I wanted her to be "comfortable." Comfort and respect would be my last gift.

As I finished lengthening the hole, the man handed me an old newspaper he had picked up from the roadside.

"You wanna cover her with this before you put the dirt in?"

"Thanks," I said, taking the paper.

I tented the paper over Gloria's body then said, "That should do it."

I made the sign of the cross and then took a handful of sand and poured it over the paper. The rattling sound of sand falling on that paper still shocks my memory.

I moved shovel after shovel of sand into the grave. In minutes, I had completed the task. I had buried misery.

The grave digger took a large, flat stone from his yard and placed it on top of the grave.

"That should keep the vermin out," the man said, up-righting himself.

I returned the shovel and said, "Thanks for digging her grave. Most people would have ignored her."

"It was the Christian thing to do," he said.

With a heavy heart, I drove away wondering what had happened to Gloria. She had walked one and a half miles from her resting place under the flowering tree to the spot where she would move no more. Who knows how long it had taken her to reach this location but why?

I presumed a combination of starvation and lack of water had motivated her to leave the shade of the tree. Perhaps, human aggression had been the motivating factor. Civilization had wrought its wrath on another helpless mound of canine flesh.

On the hot day of her death, thirst, hunger, and her health problems had been too much to endure. She had spent all her "fight."

God had done what I and the vet had failed to accomplish.

Although I grieved for her, Gloria suffered no more.

A dog is the only thing on earth that will love you more than you will love yourself.

Josh Billing

Chapter 5

Fuzzy-spots

Pow! Pow!

Gunshots echoed across the beach.

Panting, the sheriff ran past me clutching a rifle as he held onto his hat, sliding off the back of his head. He suddenly stopped, raised the weapon to his shoulder, and fired two rounds. The bullets kicked up sand near a clump of bushes four hundred feet from where I stood.

I asked myself, *Why the hell is he shooting with all these people on the beach?*

The sheriff shouted an expletive in Spanish and kicked a seashell. He turned then walked in my direction, rifle at his side.

"*Buenos Dios, Señor* Sheriff," I said. "*Que pasa?* What's up?"

"I'm after a rabid dog. Been chasing him all day, and I missed again." He chuckled then said, "I had better get in some extra firing-range time."

"Sorry you missed, Sheriff. Hope you're not giving up."

"God no! Can't let him run around and bite

someone. Don't worry. I'll get him."

Ted and Jack are two Canadians who lived near the site where the rabid dog had vanished into the bushes. For twenty-five years, each had worked in the public sector and earned a pension. Having achieved those milestones, they wanted to live in a country with a warmer climate and a lower cost of living. Their search led them to the Yucatan where they bought and renovated a beach house.

I had met the couple when I stopped by their house to inquire where they had purchased their TV satellite dish. I learned they loved dogs and had had a total of seven over twenty years—all rescued dogs.

In their Mexican home lived a small white seven-year-old male Terrier-like dog named Whitie. While not a friendly dog, no one had a reason to fear him—after all he was Canadian.

Whitie had had difficulty adjusting to Yucatan's heat and lack of grass on which to do his "business." His reluctance caused his owners so much concern they considered planting a patch of grass just so he would have a "normal" doggie bathroom. In the end, they didn't have to, but for a number of weeks, they resorted to using a piece of artificial turf, which they gradually reduced in size until all of it had been removed. It took several months for Whitie to become comfortable "using" sand instead of grass.

Late one February evening, Jack and Ted went for a stroll on the beach. Whitie accompanied them and walked quietly at full leash. He sniffed every-thing in sight while the men searched the sky for the location of the Big Dipper.

"That evening," Jack related to me, "the moon appeared so close you could almost touch it. Its legen-dary landmarks were easily seen with the naked eye.

Heat waves, rising from the day-warmed beach, disturbed the clarity of the night air causing the 'man in the moon' to 'wink' at admiring strollers."

"The moon shown so brightly," Ted told me, "One could read the fine print of a newspaper. Strollers were bathed in its light. The moonlight lent a silvery glow to everything. Thousands of tiny sea-shells, blanketing the beach, glistened like diamonds. The soft sounds of lapping waves were the only disturbance to the otherwise silent night. Stars filled the dark velvety blue-grey sky from horizon-to-horizon and sparkled like the ceiling of a Swarvoski crystal shop."

Jack said, "Let me tell Frank the rest of the story."

"There's the dipper's handle," Ted said to Jack, pointing into the northern skies over the Gulf of Mexico.

"No, that's not the handle," Jack said. "That's Orion's belt. See how close its three stars are. The dipper is farther to the right."

Ted craned his neck to search for the stars at which Jack pointed.

"Now I see it," Ted said. "You're right. The space between the handle-stars are farther apart than those of that guy's belt.'"

Jack laughed at Ted's forgetfulness, then said, "Orion."

Gusting sea breezes had waned to lighter gusts that ruffled Ted's long, reddish hair. He removed his white shirt and tied its long sleeves around his neck to better enjoy the breeze. The shirt flapped behind him like a sail on a model ship.

Jack inhaled a deep breath and exhaled a long sigh of pleasure then said, "Ahhh. This is great."

"You can say that again," Ted said.

Taking a long, deep breath, Jack said, "God, I'm

glad we live here. We couldn't dress in shorts back in Canada this time of the year."

"Nor walk on a beach."

Jack's statement about life carried great weight, for he had survived three years post-prostate-cancer surgery with no evidence of recurrence.

No longer pulling at his leash, Whitie had stopped in his path. He growled in a low pitched, foreboding voice and then barked. Suddenly, he lunged forward. He leaped with such force Ted's arm snapped to its extended position. Whitie wanted to run into the dense brush growing a hundred feet from the water's edge.

"I've never seen him pull so hard," Ted said.

"Must be a cat," Jack said.

Whitie barked, rising upright on his rear legs, causing his collar to dig into his throat. The stiffness of his neck muscles prevented him from being strangled to death.

Jack and Ted pulled at the leash, trying to calm Whitie, but he refused to be quieted. He pulled harder and harder as his bark morphed into a high pitched, strangled sound. At first, the men thought Whitie had either seen or smelled a cat, his prey of choice.

"Wouldn't a cat have run away by now?" Ted asked.

"If he had seen a cat, and it ran away, why hasn't he stopped barking?" Jack asked.

The barking continued. Whitie struggled so much the men thought he would collapse from exhaustion or asphyxiation.

Seeing nothing to be alarmed about, the men continued to walk, dragging Whitie behind them, but he refused to be quieted or walk beside the men. He barked and rose up on his back legs with such energy the men feared he would die on the spot.

"What the Hell has gotten into him?" Jack asked.

"God only knows," Ted said, continuing to drag Whitie over the damp sand. He noted the dog's paws were so dug into the sand that greater and greater amounts of energy were required to pull him forward.

"Watch out!" Ted yelled, yanking Whitie to his side.

"Why?" Jack asked. "What did you see?"

Whitie stopped barking, and the night became deadly quiet.

The men, frozen with fear, stopped in their tracks and stared into the distance. Emerging from the bushes, five hundred feet ahead, they saw a large dog romping toward them.

Shaking, Jack said, "That's got to be a heavy dog from the size of its furry body."

The approaching dog stopped and assumed a crouching position on the sand as if about to attack.

Ted whispered, "Do you hear that low, rumbling growl?"

"Shit, my heart is pounding so loud, I can't hear anything."

The intruder had multiple, ill-defined, white spots scattered throughout its dark, shaggy coat. They reflected the moonlight like safety reflectors caught in the beam of a car's headlights.

"Is it foaming at the mouth?" Jack asked.

"Stand still!" Ted shouted, picking up Whitie then holding him close to his chest.

"Don't move," Jack said in a shaky voice. "Oh my God. He's foaming at the mouth. He has rabies!"

"What are you talking about?" Ted whispered.

"Look at his mouth, damn it," Jack said, his voice filled with fear. Don't you see that . . . that foam?"

"Oh, shit!" Ted said. "Rabies!"

"Don't say that. I don't wanna hear that shit."

"What in the hell do we do now?"

Whitie squirmed so much in Ted's arms he had difficulty in restraining the dog. Whitie clawed the air with all four legs, attempting to propel himself into the intruder's domain. Whitie's barking grew to a frenzied pitch. He wanted to "get at" the intruder— despite the fact that the approaching dog was eight times Whitie's size.

The shaggy dog stopped moving forward and looped left and right, in a figure of eight, barking ferociously. Back and forth he paced like a dog in a too-small cage at the local pound. Every few seconds, the intruder would crouch then extend his front legs as if trying to go prone but afraid to do so. He barked with an interspersed low register growl.

Both kinds of sounds drove Whitie wild.

A pall of panic shrouded the men. Later, Ted would say of the situation, "I was so frightened I didn't know whether to shit or run."

The men's heart rates became more rapid than an EKG machine could track. The hair on their arms stood at attention. Nature's biochemistry of "fight or flight" had reached its zenith.

"What the hell do we do?" Ted asked.

"I think we should get the hell out of here," Jack replied.

"If we run, that damn dog will come after us. Hold on a minute," Ted said, patting the air with a shaking hand in an effort to calm Jack. "Damn it. Let's think."

"Shit! He's coming this way," Jack said, fear choking his words.

"He's not going to stop 'til he gets us," Ted said, in a quivering voice. "Maybe we should just stand still, no eye contact."

"God!" Jack said. "You think he'll just go away."

"You're kidding," Ted said, the pitch of his voice rising. "That damn dog is after *us*. He's not going away. I can see it in his eyes."

The growling dog crept forward then stopped. He stood upright for a moment then crouched, slinking back and forth while barking and flashing his fangs. The foam hanging from his jowls glistened like a movie marquee advertising danger as his growling became more menacing.

Jack stooped and fingered a half-buried, fist-sized piece of broken concrete near his right foot. With seawater dripping from the would-be missile, he pulled the craggy fragment from the sand then gripped it in his trembling hand.

"This is our protection," Jack whispered, righting himself while holding the concrete with a death grip. His hands visibly shook.

The growling dog, head held low, stopped three-hundred-feet away and paced left and right in a menacing fashion.

Whitie's squirming and barking persisted, but his thready, raspy bark now sounded like he had laryngitis.

Ted gripped Whitie's snout and lower jaw to silence him as he hugged the dog to his chest. Whitie gave an occasional squirm, trying to extricate his head from Ted's grip but to no avail.

"Quiet," Ted whispered to Whitie.

Picking up another piece of concrete, Jack whispered to Ted, "Start walking backwards toward the house—slowly. I'll do the same but keep an eye on that dog."

The threatening dog crept forward then stood erect two-hundred-feet from the men. The dog growled as it paused. He crouched, his chin touching the sand, and barked. He growled as if giving a final warning before attacking. The dog's foamy saliva had increased in mass and length and dripped in a clump onto the sand.

"In a second, I'm going to tell you to run home," Jack said. "Get ready."

"I'm so scared I don't know if I can fuckin' move," Ted whimpered.

Ted crept backed toward home.

Suddenly, Jack yelled, "Run!"

Ted turned and ran as fast as he could over the hard-packed sand. Filled with fear, he gasped for air. His breath came hard and fast, sounding like a steam locomotive attacking a steep grade.

Whitie's head jostled about like a bobble-head doll. Ted pressed the dog's head against his chest to prevent its neck from breaking. Whitie must have sensed something amiss because he became silent.

Ted bounded over the moonlit sand like a grasshopper skimming over a sun-heated asphalt road. Occasionally, Ted yelled in pain as he stepped, barefooted, on broken seashells. Behind him, he heard Jack yell, "Run Ted! Run!"

Exhausted and panting hard, Ted neared the corroded gate and rusty chain-link fence surrounding his yard. The salt air had taken its toll on the fence, its galvanized posts, and gate.

Like a man with disabling arthritis, Ted fumbled with the gate's unyielding latch. Finally, the latch surrendered to a hard kick, and the gate swung open. Ted hurled himself into the safety of the fenced yard like a linebacker rushing the end zone for a touchdown. Whitie fell free as Ted hit the sand. Catching his breath, Ted slammed the gate closed then stood up. "Thank you, God," he muttered. "I made it." Bent over, he placed his hands on his knees, panting. He looked left, watching Jack racing home.

Ted didn't know the stray dog had diverted its course and had chased him as he scampered toward home. He might have imagined such a scene, but he didn't know it had happened.

Thanks to Jack's throwing a piece of concrete at the dog, it veered from its path of mauling Ted and ran into a stand of bushes.

Not knowing if the dog would resume its pursuit, Jack continued his exhausting run for the safety of his enclosed front yard. Every few seconds, he glanced over his shoulder to see if the dog pursued him.

Suddenly, a cramp squeezed his right calf muscle. With every step, the pain mounted until it became excruciating. He started to limp and wanted to stop running but knew he couldn't—not then. The muscle felt like it had been crushed by an anvil, but Jack continued to stumble forward. Almost falling on his face, he caught his balance then resumed the run of his life.

I've got to keep going.

Ted had caught his breath and stood ready to open the gate as soon as Jack arrived.

As Jack neared the yard, Ted tried to open the gate, but the earlier slamming-jolt, plus gravity, had caused the gate's latch to fall into the locked and stuck position.

"Shit!" Ted yelled, pulling at the latch.

"Open the damn gate!" Jack yelled.

Using his last ounce of strength and a sharp kick with his barefoot, the latch yielded. Ted threw open the gate just in time for Jack to stumble through the opening.

Exhaustion and leg pain brought him face down on the sand but safe. As he writhed on the ground, he clutched his cramping calf and yelled, "Shit! Shit!"

Almost in a panic, and with the assistance of Ted's outstretched hand, Jack pulled himself halfway erect. He forced himself to limp farther into the yard.

Ted closed the gate while Jack wiped sand from

his face. The men then collapsed, side-by-side on the sand, recovering from the physiological effects of their escape.

Jack chuckled. "I think I shit my pants."

"You didn't," Ted said.

"No, but I almost did."

Exhaustion prevented them from pushing Whitie away as he licked their faces.

After a few minutes of panting and sighing, the men forced themselves upright then walked to the porch where they fell into their favorite chairs. Facing the sea, the men pondered their escape from death.

After a few minutes of reflection, Jack said, "That was close."

"Too close," Ted said, in halting speech. "I hope that son-of-a-bitch, has gone off somewhere to die."

"And soon," Jack said, slumping into his chair cushion. Moments later, he said, "I'm going to take a shower and go to bed."

"I won't be far behind you," Jack said and then yawned, "but first, I need a Scotch."

Ted carried his morning mug of Colombian brew to the front porch then sat down in his favorite chair. He took a sip of joe and looked across the mirror-like surface of the Gulf of Mexico. Suddenly, he yelled, "Oh my god!" *I can't believe this.*

"What is it?" Jack called from the second floor.

"That son-of-a-bitching dog that chased us is blocking the front gate."

Ted began to shake. He placed his jiggling mug on a nearby table. The ceramic cup met the table top with a loud thud, spilling a few drops of java in the process.

The beach dog looked in the direction of the noise as Ted ran yelling into the house. "Jack! Jack!

Get down here, now!"

"What's wrong?" Jack yelled, from upstairs.

Ted heard Jack thump across the span of the second-floor bedroom as he hurried toward the stairs.

Upon reaching the bottom step, Jack rubbed sleep from his eyes, pulled at his boxers, and asked, "Why are you yelling?"

Holding his finger to his lips, Ted pointed out the door and whispered, "Shhh. Look at the gate."

Jack walked on tip toes toward the opened patio doors and peered in the direction of Ted's pointing.

"There, on the sand . . . in front of the gate," Ted said. "It's that damn dog that chased us last night."

The dog had either seen or smelled the men because it turned its head toward them and sniffed the air.

Jack asked, "What do you think it's doing here?"

"Maybe he's back for a second try at taking a bite out of us," Ted said then chuckled. Pointing toward the dog's wagging tail, he asked, "What do you think that wagging means?"

"Damned if I know," Jack said, shrugging.

Neither a friendly nor an angry type of wag, the dog's tail moved in a narrow arc as it dragged across the sand. With its head cocked to the left, the dog rose to a sitting position, whined, and then started to pant.

Both men noted the dog no longer foamed at the mouth.

Making a noisy appearance on the porch, Whitie pushed his way between the men's bare feet. He seemed ready to pounce on the shaggy dog, however, he never left his owners' side. He barked with a raspy voice as his tail arched over his hips and the hair on his spine stood erect. The hoarseness of his bark had no doubt resulted from his vocal protests the evening before.

The shaggy dog returned Whitie's barks, while

wagging its tail.

Jack, and then Ted nudged Whitie with their feet and yelled, "Quiet! Shut up!"

Whitie refused to stop barking. Ted picked him up, placed him in the house, and then closed the patio door. Not dissuaded by captivity, Whitie scratched at the glass door in an attempt to get at the stray lying at the gate. Even in confinement, Whitie continued to protest the stray's presence.

The stray dog, apparently no longer feeling threatened, quieted down. He stood at the gate, panting, and wagging his tail.

The guys began a heated discussion over what to do about the unwanted stray.

"Do we know anyone who owns a gun?" Ted asked.

"Hell, I don't, and besides, possessing a gun would be illegal."

"Maybe we should call the sheriff. This could be the dog he was chasing, and he has a rifle."

"You know he's not going to come here for a stray dog," Jack said.

"Let's tell him it has rabies. What do we have to lose? He wouldn't even have to get out of his Jeep. Just shoot the damn thing."

Ted left to get his cell phone. Moments later, he returned to the porch with the phone held to his ear. "It's ringing," he said. Ted mouthed the word "ring" at the sound of each ring at the other end. After several rings, Ted said, "He's not answering. That's weird; his voicemail isn't picking up either."

"Well, we can't just stand here," Jack said, in an anger-tinged voice.

"What do you expect *me* to do?"

Jack patted the air. "Calm down. We need to put on our thinking-caps. Just sit down and think for a minute, will ya?"

Jack went to a storage room and searched through boxes of books he had brought from Canada. The boxes had not been unpacked due to the *mañana* attitude the men had adopted since arriving in Mexico.

After searching through three boxes, Jack found a biology book from his college days. Thumbing through the index, he found the word *Rabies*. He turned to page 494 then searched for the heading *RABIES*. His finger moved down the page while he mouthed the words he read, *Etiology*, *Signs and Symptoms*, *Clinical Course*.

With his index finger on the page containing the text concerning rabies, he closed the book then hurried to the porch where Ted still pondered a course of action.

"Look," Jack said, pointing to the book. "Look at this. Here's the information I wanted. Have a look." Jack opened the book and pointed at line twelve. "It says '… rabies causes hydrophobia or fear of water.'"

Jack brought his index finger down with a thud on page 297. "But listen up," he said, starting to read the next line.

Prodromal period (stage l) - first 1 to 3 days after the rabies virus reaches the central nervous system, vague neurologic signs appear then progress rapidly.

Excitative stage (stage 2) - next 2 to 3 days. This is the "furious" stage – even tame animals suddenly become vicious, attacking other animals (and at times humans) as the animal roams and wanders.

Paralytic stage (stage 3) - follows stage 2. The throat and chewing muscles become

paralyzed; the animal is unable to swallow
and drools excessively. The lower jaw may
drop. Death usually occurs within 10 days
after stage I.

After reading the information, the men decided to
offer the stray some food. They reasoned a rabid dog
would not only refuse water but food as well. They
re-read the selected page:

A rabid dog's rejection of food and water is
due to the inability to swallow, secondary to
paralysis and destruction of the nervous
system. In such circumstances, eating or
drinking is impossible.

The men chose dog biscuits as their experimental
tool. They could be thrown and thus avoid the risks
involved in getting close to the dog.

Ted took a few biscuits from Whitie's stash of
goodies in a bowl beside the patio door. The job of
throwing them fell to Jack. He had played baseball in
his youth and had been known for his "mean hook"
and "spitball."

Fingering the irregular, hard treat, Jack took
careful aim and then threw it toward the dog. The
treat sailed in a low-angle arc, just clearing the top of
the gate, then fell within eighteen inches of the dog.
The startled animal ran as if he had been hit by a
rock.

The men had not expected the dog to be so
frightened by a thrown biscuit. Nevertheless, they
waited several minutes, hoping the dog would
become curious and leave his safety zone at water's
edge. Even better, eat the treat.

After staring at the men for a few minutes, the
dog sniffed the air then approached the treat. Sniffing

the sand and the air with caution, he moved closer and closer to the treat. With one last sniff of the air, the dog took the treat in its mouth. After two loud crunches, the treat went "south."

"Now, what do we do?" Jack asked.

Unsure of the status of the dog's health, the men decided to offer more treats.

They discussed whether or not the dog might have been so hungry it forced itself to eat despite mouth or throat pain.

"Does this mean it *doesn't* have rabies?" Ted asked.

"Maybe, but maybe paralysis hasn't set in—*yet*."

Jack walked toward the living room. He opened the patio door, and using his bare foot to prevent Whitie from bolting from the house, he entered the building and then closed the door. Moments later, he returned to the porch with a handful of treats. This time, Ted would feed the dog.

Gripping a few treats, Ted walked barefooted over the warm sand toward the crouching dog. Ted didn't have the pitcher's arm of Jack, so to ensure the treat reached its target, he walked closer to the dog than he wanted. He stopped about twenty feet from the panting, tail-wagging threat. He knew the dog had smelled the treats, for it moved closer to the gate.

Ted threw a treat. His pitch was right-on in that it sailed, unimpeded, through one of the diamond shaped openings of the chain link fence and fell at the dog's feet.

As the treat hit the sand, Ted exclaimed, "It went just the way I wanted."

"Sure it did," Jack said, chuckling. "Who taught you to throw like a girl?"

The dog sniffed and then took the treat into its mouth. Crunch, crunch and it disappeared.

Ted tossed several more treats.

In seconds, all were gobbled up. After eight treats, the dog seemed to smack its lips.

"I'm out of treats," Ted yelled, "and my pitching arm is sore. If you want the damn dog to have more, you'll have to throw 'em. I'm not."

Jack laughed. "I don't think it needs anymore."

"I'm beginning to think the dog does *not* have rabies."

"If it doesn't, why did it chase us," Jack asked, and why did it foam at the mouth?"

With a questioning look at each other, the men retreated to the shade of the porch, sat in their hammock chairs, and watched the dog at their gate.

"Could it be the dog didn't chase *us*?" Ted asked. "Whitie is a much smaller dog, but he's the one who started barking."

The more the men discussed their dog, the more plausible it seemed Whitie had been the stray dog's target—not the men.

"*If*—and a big *if*—that was the case, what are we going to do?" Jack asked.

After more discussion, the men thought they would approach the dog and observe his reaction. With some reticence, the barefooted men crept, side-by-side, toward the gate. The prone dog looked at them for a second then tilted its head—first right, then left. The men crept closer. The dog remained prone and stared at the approaching men with squinted eyes. The guys were three inches from the gate when the dog suddenly jumped to a standing position.

Startled, the men jumped backwards. Ted almost fell. Dumbfounded, they watched the dog put its nose through one of the diamond shaped openings in the gate and make a muffled whining sound.

"Think this means he's hungry for affection or just hungry?" Ted chuckled.

"Maybe both," Jack said, "but he could be in

pain, or maybe his bark was muffled because of the gate wire surrounding his snout."

The men stepped back from the gate and stared at the dog.

"I think he's okay," Ted said.

"I wouldn't be so sure."

"Why not? Since when did we become experts on canine behavior or rabies?"

"I'm not saying I'm an expert," Jack quipped, "but I don't believe it has rabies. Besides, I've got something else in mind."

Confronting the stray constituted only one part of the rabies-elimination-testing Jack had in mind.

"What would happen, if we approached the dog while carrying Whitie?" Jack asked. "I'll, hold him the way we did last night . . . prevent him from being injured."

"Yeah. We don't want an in-your-face confrontation between the two," Ted said. "Sounds good. Let's do it."

After a few minutes inside, Jack had prepared Whitie. A leash dangled from his rhinestone collar. The hand-loop of the leash was around Jack's right wrist. If Whitie got free, he could not go far.

Jack backed out of the patio doors to block each dog's view of the other. With Whitie clutched against his chest, Jack walked backwards down the steps toward the gate as Whitie squirmed to get free. Expecting Whitie might bark, Jack clamped his hand around the dog's snout and continued backing toward the gate.

Ted walked to the right of Jack's path, in part, to block Whitie's view and to help Jack keep on track.

Two feet from the gate, and still clutching Whitie, Jack turned to confront the spotted stray. He barked aggressively and clawed the fence. Whitie managed to free his snout from Jack's grip and joined in the cacophony. The little dog squirmed, trying to wrest himself from Jack's embrace.

The spotted dog jumped up and down, pawed the gate, and barked loud enough to wake the dead.

The barking had continued for several seconds when Ted yelled, "Take Whitie in the house!"

It seemed clear to the guys the spotted dog had eyes only for Whitie—not them.

With Whitie confined to the house, the men sat on the porch.

"What about the dog's foaming mouth?" Ted asked.

"What about it?"

"What caused it?"

"Damned if I know!"

"One reason could be rabies," Jack asserted.

One theory gained prominence and seemed most likely. The men theorized the dog had been without water for a long time and was dehydrated. That was not an uncommon occurrence among stray dogs during the dry season. Rainfall had been zilch. There were no rain puddles to drink from, and there were few people at the beach who might have provided water for stray animals. If the dog was dehydrated, then its saliva would become concentrated—thickened.

Given these conditions, panting and barking could cause saliva to foam and present itself as the sign most often associated with rabies. Perhaps, the guys thought, this explained the dog's rabid appearance.

While the guys had no doubts the spotted dog would drink water, they wanted to see for themselves. Jack took Whitie's water bowl, washed it, filled it with tap water, and then carried it to the front porch.

"Ted," Jack called, "talk to the dog so he's

distracted. I'm going to put this bowl outside the fence . . . near the house?"

"Where?" Jack asked.

"Near the house but far from where the dog is now."

To distract the stray from Jack's actions, Ted knelt two feet away from the dog and whispered, "Good doggie. Good doggie."

Jack stretched himself over the fence, careful not to spill the water. The bowl was settled into the sand with a twisting motion then Jack moved to the shade of the porch. He called to Ted, "See if you can get the dog to follow you along the fence to the water bowl."

While saying "doggie" and quietly snapping his fingers, Ted coaxed the stray along the outside perimeter of the fence, toward the bowl of water.

At first, the dog ignored the water. Ted squatted on the sand, opposite the bowl, and attempted to draw the dog's attention to the water. After a few attempts, the dog discovered the liquid. He drank as if he had not had water in weeks. He didn't stop to catch his breath until the bowl was empty.

"That's one thirsty dog!" Jack yelled. "I feel a lot better about him now that I've seen him drink water."

"One thing we know for sure . . . he doesn't have hydrophobia," Ted said.

The men felt a sense of relief. They were ninety percent certain the dog did not have rabies. However, the question arose as to what they should do with or about the stray. They could not take him in because of the animosity between it and Whitie.

They decided to ignore it.

For a few days, they didn't feed it or offer it water. Nevertheless, the dog came and went.

Often, it would lay belly down in the sand at the front gate and stay there for varying amounts of time. If Whitie didn't discover the intruder, the stray might hang around for an hour or more.

The guys were happy the stray didn't hang about for longer periods of time. Perhaps, they believed, the dog was finding food and water somewhere else. This relieved them of unspoken guilt for not being more benevolent toward the needy animal.

A few weeks after Ted's and Jack's first encounter with the stray, they noticed it had a bloated belly. At first, they thought the dog suffered from food deprivation or had starvation due to intestinal parasites. For a few days, they tried to ignore the dog and its bloated belly.

One morning, while Ted enjoyed his morning coffee on the porch, he noticed what he thought were teats on the stray. Its shaggy coat made it difficult to fully evaluate the stray's abdomen but the dog appeared to have teats.

"Oh my god, the dog's pregnant," Ted said.

Until this time, the men had referred to the dog as *it* or *he,* but now, Ted knew *he* was a *she.*

Ted turned to Jack as he stepped onto the porch, carrying his cup of morning joe.

"I think *he* is a *she* and she is pregnant." Ted pointed out his findings. "She's getting tits."

Jack took note and settled into a cushy, porch chair. Sipping his coffee, he said, "So? What do you want me to do?"

After a moment of deep thought, Ted said, "Maybe we should feed her."

Swallowing hard, Jack said, "If *you* want to feed her go ahead but feed her far from the house. I don't want Whitie getting all worked up over seeing her, or we'll have no peace or quiet around here. The two will be barking all the time."

"The gestational period for puppies is nine weeks," Ted said, "and this stray has to be about five or maybe six weeks pregnant. If I'm right, there's still time to feed her everything she needs to assure she has healthy puppies."

"Yeah, but first you have to find a safe place to feed her."

The guys discussed several feeding spots near the house then decided on the safety of the bushes that grew about thirty feet to the west of their driveway

Needing something with which to feed the dog, now named Fuzzy Spots, Jack and Ted went shopping for dog food and bowls.

The *bodega* in nearby Progreso had a good selection of dry dog food. There, the men purchased a bag of puppy food. It contained more calories, protein, and nutrients than adult dog food. They also chose red plastic bowls for the dog's food and water. The color would be easily seen in the shade of the bushes where Fuzzy Spots was to be fed.

The guys left the store whistling and then smiling.

"We're going to have babies. We're going to have babies," Ted chanted as he drove home.

Until then, the men had not touched the stray. They had been reluctant to do so for fear of rabies, but they believed if the dog had had rabies, it would now be dead.

Since she wasn't dead, she didn't have rabies. Conscious of this fact, they decided they would approach the dog outside the protection of their fence.

When the men returned home, the dog was nowhere to be seen. They weren't worried, for they knew she would return. Sure enough, an hour later, the dog appeared at the front gate. Even though Ted and Jack were enjoying Margaritas on the porch, they placed their drinks on a table and went into the house to get food and water for Fuzzy Spots.

They left the house through the back door and crossed the driveway behind their forty-foot-long recreational vehicle (RV), parked in the narrow, sandy space that was their side yard. Ted whistled and called to the dog still at the front gate.

Fuzzy Spot's ears jutted skyward, and she turned her head toward Ted.

Ted whistled.

The dog started walking toward the men. She turned the corner of the fence and continued her stroll. The closer she got to the men, the slower she moved.

Ted asked, "Do you think the absence of the fence between us is causing her to feel insecure.

"You think she is afraid of us?" Jack whispered.

"Who knows?"

The dog continued to walk toward Ted until she was about fifteen feet away. She stopped, stood still, and then stared straight ahead. Ted, carrying the bowl of water, moved cautiously toward her. She backed away. He hadn't expected that reaction, so he backed away as Jack joined the retreat. Appearing wary, the dog stared at them.

The men agreed they should take their bowls into the bushes and hoped the dog would follow them to the designated feeding area.

Jack, followed by Ted, pushed his way into the shadows of the bushes, careful not to spill food or water. They found a small clearing about twenty feet into the bushes where they placed their bowls on the sand. They then backtracked, breaking off a few branches to ease their way through the foliage.

As they exited the bushes, they noted the dog had moved closer to where they had entered the under-brush.

Ted, leading the way, went back to the driveway

where he stooped to see the leaves of the bushes were sparse near the ground, giving the men an unobstructed sightline to the bowls. This meant the men would be able to watch the dog eat and drink from the comfort of their rear patio. The men sat down in patio chairs and waited for the dog to find the bowls.

Tired of waiting, Ted walked toward the rear of the RV where he got down on all fours and peered under the vehicle. He could see the dog's lower legs on the other side. He watched her inch forward.

She soon moved into Jack's sightline. "I can see her."

Ted righted himself. Moaning, he rubbed his right hand on his lower back. "I'm getting too old for this kneeling and praying stuff."

Half-bent over, Ted limped to the patio then sat beside Jack where they watched the dog follow its sniffing nose into the bushes.

She sniffed every inch of the path the men had taken until she was about two feet from the bowls. She stopped, smelled the ground and then looked toward her benefactors. She re-sniffed the ground and crept toward the bowls. After sniffing the water, she lapped it. Her thirst greater than her hunger. Moments later, she ate the food. The sound of its crunching could be heard at the patio.

Having had her fill, she walked around the bowls and moved farther into the bush where she made a few nesting circles then curled up on the sand. Within a few minutes, she appeared to sleep.

The guys were disappointed they couldn't pet Fuzzy Spots, but they were happy she was eating proper food and they were one step closer to owning another dog and who knew how many puppies.

Over the next few weeks, they repeated the feeding ritual twice daily. Fuzzy Spots would not permit her patrons to pet her. When called, she wagged her tail but kept her distance. She often retreated to the shade of the bushes that had become her home. The

The men knew the dog's delivery date grew near because she spent less and less time away from her adopted home.

One morning, Ted went to feed her. "Jack!" he yelled. "She isn't here."

Even though Fuzzy Spots wasn't anywhere to be seen, Ted left her food, believing she would soon return. Every hour or so, during the morning, both men scanned the yard, hoping to see her.

At lunch time, Ted knelt on his back patio to see the red bowls under the bushes. *She's not there. Better see if anything has been eaten.*

Much to his horror, the food and water were un-touched except for a green bug that had crawled in and drowned.

Concerned for Fuzzy Spots safety, Ted shared his findings with Jack. They decided she had gone to some protected place to deliver her pups. They would have to wait for her to decide when it was safe to return.

The following day, Ted examined the bowls. The food was still there, but the water bowl contained five drowned bugs. Sadly, the water level had not chang-ed, meaning their dog had not been drinking.

When weather permitted, the men ate lunch on the front porch. There, they could enjoy a view of the gulf and its cool breezes as they ate. However, on that particular day, a *Norte* storm blew in from the Gulf of Mexico. The storm blew sand everywhere, making dining on the porch impossible, so the guys ate on the back patio. There they would be protected from the wind and enjoy their alfresco lunch minus the crunch of sand.

Strong gusts of wind lifted the red checkered

tablecloth, so Jack secured it with heavy seashells. He then set the table and filled glasses with iced tea. While he waited for his favorite food, Ted warmed leftover barbecued ribs from the night before.

"Wow, that's a lot of food!" Jack said as Ted placed a platter of ribs on the table. "Didn't know you had cooked so much."

Jack loaded his plate with the meaty ribs then passed the platter to Ted. The men ate in silence, except for an occasional "yum."

With a mouth half-filled and sauce on his lips, Jack asked, "Did you hear that?"

"What?" Ted asked. "What did you hear?"

"I'm not sure. Be quiet for a minute."

The men stopped chewing and listened. They heard nothing.

"Maybe it was the wind," Ted said. "It's blowing stronger than fifteen minutes ago."

"Yeah, maybe the wind."

The men turned their attention to the heap of ribs and enjoyed lunch. Two ribs later, Jack said, "I did hear something. There it is again. I'm going to look."

Wiping sauce from his fingers, Jack walked toward the bushes. On the way, he passed the rear of the RV. As he approached the vehicle, he became convinced he heard a strange sound coming from beneath it. Clutching his aching knees, he got on all fours then peered into the shadows under the vehicle. While it took a moment for his eyes to dark adapt, he heard a strange sound. Despite the low clearance of the undercarriage he saw a mound-like object, and it moved.

Jack yelled, "Ted, come here!"

Ted ran to the RV where he too got on all fours and peered into the shadows. "Oh … my … God. It's the dog … She's had her puppies."

The men watched for as long as their aching knees would allow. Jack got up and walked around the RV to Ted's position and helped him up.

"Congratulations, *Daddy*," Jack said and slapped Ted on the back.

"Congratulations to you too, *Daddy*," Ted said and hugged Jack.

They returned to the patio and their lunch of ribs.

Much to their surprise, Fuzzy Spots crawled from under the RV and approached the patio. The men stopped eating and faced the dog. She inched closer, her head down, and her tail tucked between her legs. Not knowing what to expect, the guys moved off the patio and knelt, in the sand, a few feet from the dog. Fuzzy Spots moved forward but stopped about eighteen inches from the men.

"Hello, girl," Ted said, extending his hand to pet her. As he reached out, Fuzzy raised her head under his palm. Ted extended his fingers and caressed her head.

"Wow!" Ted exclaimed. "We've made contact."

Jack scratched behind her right ear. She whined, extended her tucked tail and wagged it. The ice had been broken. She had accepted her benefactors.

The men were overcome with joy.

"She must be very hungry to leave her pups," Ted said.

"Whoopee!" Jack yelled, causing Fuzzy Spots to jerk backward and retreat several inches.

"You frightened her," Ted said, waving toward the dog.

Jack returned to the table and selected the rib with the most meat. Not knowing how the dog would react to a sauce containing tomatoes, sugar, and vinegar, he scraped away as much sauce as possible. He then presented the rib to Fuzzy Spots. Her tail wagged furiously, creating a small breeze. She snatched the rib from his hand then retreated to the protection of the RV's undercarriage.

"How long do you think she's gone without food or water?" Ted asked.

"God only knows, but she looked okay."

Jack retrieved the dog's bowls, scattering the old food throughout the bushes then poured the water and dead bugs onto the sand. He took the bowls to the kitchen, washed and dried them then refilled each.

"Ted," Jack yelled, "will ya get the broom from the storage closet and bring it to the RV?"

"Will do," Ted said, holding the screen door open for Jack. "Don't want you spilling anything."

Ted took the broom to Jack who waited at the side of the RV. He placed the bowls on the sand, and using the bristle end of the broom, he pushed them under the vehicle. "There," Jack said, "she can have food and water without leaving the pups."

The guys reveled in their new parental status.

Over the next two weeks, they spent many minutes lying on their bellies in the sand, observing the pups nestled against their mother.

Fuzzy Spots ate so much the men increased her feedings to four a day. Even so, her bowls were always empty.

The pups were sometimes observed with the aid of a flashlight. To increase their viewing pleasure, the men purchased a second flashlight, so both men could observe the pups waddle about their den. Most often, the pups nursed or slept.

Ted and Jack kept their distance from the pups, fearing Fuzzy Spots would not permit them to get closer. Ted, however, wanted to see the pups up close. Since he was the thinner man, he would crawl partway under the RV and have a look at the pups. However, crawling brought his butt in contact with the RV's undercarriage, making full exploration impossible.

"Damn, my fat ass," Ted said. "I can't do this."

Jack laughed at Ted's predicament. "I told you. You need to lose weight."

With grease covering the backside of his shorts, Ted squirmed from under the vehicle. Not to be deterred, he pondered what he might do. Minutes later, he had a eureka moment—he would dig a trench under the RV. It would give him not only more headroom but butt room as well.

He hoped Fuzzy Spots would not perceive the digging activity as a threat to her pups.

Having located their long-handle shovel, Ted returned to the RV then used the shovel to drag sand from under the vehicle.

On his knees, Jack stared under the RV and observed the excavation project. "God, I hope that doesn't frighten her," he muttered as Ted shoveled.

During the digging, Fuzzy Spots watched, tilting her head first left and then right but made no threatening moves or sounds.

Ten minutes was all the time Ted needed to excavate a trench deep enough to permit his butt to pass below the undercarriage.

With the shovel out of the way, and flashlight in hand, Ted crawled toward the puppies. He inched closer and closer to Fuzzy Spots. "Okay doggie. I'm not going to hurt you or your pups."

As Ted got closer, Fuzzy Spots inched backwards. "She's not doing much of anything," Ted called to Jack, "She backed up a bit, but she's not growling or doing anything threatening."

Quietly, Ted called to Jack, "Hold my ankles and get ready to pull me out of here if I'm attacked."

Ted pushed the butt of his flashlight into the Sand and aimed its beam toward the underside of the vehicle. The reflected light illuminated the nursery. He felt compelled to touch one of the little bundles of fur. Keeping one eye on the mother and the other on the pups, Ted extended his hand toward the nearest puppy. For a moment, his hand was motionless.

Fuzzy Spots remained still and silent. Ted's hand inched closer to a puppy then paused again. Still, Fuzzy Spots remained motionless and quiet.

Hand trembling, Ted extended his index finger over a pup's head. *Everything is going to be okay.*

Fuzzy Spots made a rumbling, guttural sound, and Ted recoiled, bumping his head against the underframe. He retracted his arm so fast his elbow dug into the sand, knocking enough sand onto his face to create a dune.

"Damn!" Ted said, spitting sand.

"What's wrong?" Jack yelled, tugging on Ted's ankles.

"Don't pull! I *think* she growled, but I'm not sure. I don't know what to do."

"Maybe you should get out—try later," Jack said, applying additional tension to Ted's ankles.

"No, not yet. I want to stay here a little longer. Let her to get used to my being here."

"Are you sure?"

"Yeah, but I'll come back tomorrow and try petting the pups then."

"*What* are you going to try tomorrow?"

"Pet the pups," Ted said.

"Let well enough alone. Get out of there."

"Ease up on my ankles," Ted yelled. "I'm going to try something."

Using his elbows, Ted pushed himself forward until he was close enough to touch all the pups. Inch by inch, he extended his hand toward one puppy then paused. His hand then moved closer, paused, and then reached the top of the pup's head. In a flash, Fuzzy

Spots extended her open mouth toward Ted's hand, whined, and then licked his fingers.

"Oh my god!" Ted yelled.

"What happened?" Jack yelled, pulling on Ted's legs.

"Stop pulling! I'm okay. She licked my finger. I *thought* she was going to bite me, but she didn't. She licked me and let me touch a puppy."

Ted had touched the pup's head, using as little pressure as possible. He then caressed its head and sensed the pleasure the puppy experienced. Ted had experienced pleasure by giving pleasure. The other puppies continued to sleep as Ted's finger found its way from puppy head to puppy head.

Fuzzy Spots had accepted Ted presence. With his mission accomplished, and a heart bursting with joy, Ted asked Jack to help extract the happy man from the undercarriage.

Once Ted had cleared the vehicle's underside, he stood and brushed sand from his clothes. He smiled so broadly sunlight sparkled on the gold crown of a rear molar.

"How many males and females are there?" Jack asked.

"Oh my god! I didn't think to look."

"How could you forget a thing like that?"

"I was too happy and busy petting little heads." Ted grinned. "Besides, I didn't want to press my luck by picking them up."

Over the following weeks, the men watched the puppies grow and romp about the sandy yard. They often had difficulty walking on the shifting sand. If they wandered too far from the RV, Fuzzy Spots mouthed them by the nap of the neck and stopped the pup's possible encounter with danger.

After a couple of months, Fuzzy Spots soon felt

she could leave the RV for long periods of time, perhaps for an amorous rendezvous or to seek rest from her suckling pups.

It wasn't long after she started to leave the safety of the RV that the pups followed her. The sight of the furry puppies, stumbling in slow pursuit of their mother, brought the men great joy.

Although eager to explore their new world, the puppies were not ready to leave their mother's side. Even though they might stumble over each other as they rolled behind her, they never had difficulty in finding a teat at feeding time.

At twelve weeks of age, each pup was placed in a forever-home with adoring children to care for them.

At the appropriate time, all were "fixed."

Fuzzy Spots was also spayed. While she couldn't have more puppies, one could tell she loved the ones she had. Two of her pups lived close enough that they would visit their mother from time to time.

Fuzzy Spots now lives as an indoor dog with Ted, Jack, and Whitie who has accepted her presence.

The two dogs can often be seen walking and playing on the beach.

Both dogs have their rabies inoculations updated regularly.

Animals and nature are insignificant for a man when the man is unworthy.

Anonymous

Chapter 6

MTB
(Mother-To-Be)

I stomped on the brake pedal. The tires screeched, the rear of the car rose off the ground, and I was jettisoned forward. My chest ached from being pressed against the seat belt while my head snapped forward, striking the sun visor. Several items on the passenger seat, obeying the law of inertia, took flight and struck the dash-board.

"Damn it!" I said, gripping the steering wheel so hard one would have thought I was trying to choke it to death. I loosened my grip and stretched my fingers. My hands shook, and my heart raced as I moved the gear shift to park.

A short, young emaciated female dog scampered from in front of my car, ran onto the north shoulder of the road, and then disappeared into the underbrush.

"You're awfully young to be out here alone, little doggie. Bet your mother is dead."

Exhaling a long sigh of relief, I, unlike many drivers in the Yucatan, had avoided killing a stray dog, but I felt emotionally and physically wrung out over the near miss. My heart raced and my vision seemed blurred.

Gradually, I returned to a nearly normal mental and physical state of being.

I often traveled this road, and I was always vigilant about stray dogs near the garbage dump where I had just stopped, but I had never before seen the dog I almost killed.

Another unwanted stray, I thought. *God knows where they come from.*

Opposite the underbrush, into which the dog disappeared, stood the local self-service garbage dump. The dump was an unofficial disposal site for those who could not, or chose not to, pay for garbage pickup at their home.

Residential pickup had been available in Yucatan for years but cost $5.00 U.S. dollars a month. The cost was considered excessive by poorer locals for whom ten U.S. dollars was a day's pay. This expense caused many locals to throw their trash along the shoulder of roads.

Dump-trash was supposed to be placed in plastic bags and left in the middle of the free site where government trucks would collect it every three to four weeks. However, the plastic bag rule was often ignored, creating an aesthetic eyesore and ecological insult.

A small shack, constructed of cardboard and metal, sat in the middle of the dump. Inside, a volunteer attendant avoided the sun while waiting for clients needing assistance in unloading trash from their vehicle. The attendant expected pocket change, equaling fifteen to twenty cents (U.S.), for his help. These attendants attempted to corral the garbage to prevent it from being strewn about by rummaging animals or blown across adjacent fields. However, attendants were not always present or caring.

Ecologically unconcerned people often left trash in inappropriate containers. These would be raided by packs of dogs, cats, and other animals that tore into the bundles, leaving the contents to scavenger birds, iguanas, opossums, rats, lizards, and the whims of the winds.

The dog, I had almost killed, had no doubt been scavenging in the dump. I doubted she found much to eat, for there wasn't much garbage that morning.

Down the road, toward the east, I noted three stray dogs making their way toward the dump. I watched them approach and then cross in front of my car while the last bit of near-death stress drained from my body. I redirected the dashboard's vent and its cooling zephyr toward my face. It helped me relax. I then resumed my drive toward Chelem.

Several days later, I passed the dump. Pawing at a trash-stuffed plastic bag, I saw the black and brown spotted dog I had almost killed days earlier. I parked at the side of the road and observed her for a few seconds.

She was the thinnest living dog I had ever seen. Her lack of fat and muscle tissue allowed me to see all her bones. Almost to the point of ripping, her spotted coat was stretched taunt by starvation. She had scattered patches of hair loss but no evidence of the dreaded red mange I had come to know through care of strays. I noted she didn't have a "boated belly" so often seen in stray dogs. Why she didn't I don't know. Most dogs scavenging the dump had mange and protein-robbing parasites. The apparent absence of these findings in this dog meant she was not dying yet—but close.

I lowered my window and whistled. The dog stopped her search for a moment, turned, and looked in my direction. I took some dog treats from my glove box then tossed them in her direction. Swoosh. The treat sailed through the air and landed within finding distance of the dog but not too close to frighten her as they hit the ground.

Startled, she gathered herself up like an accordian preparing to take in air if the situation warranted flight. She stared in my direction leaving me with the feeling we had made contact.

"Please don't run away. If you do, another dog will get your food."

She raised her nose and sniffed the air.

"Go. Get the food," I whispered. "Find the food."

Having smelled the treat, she appeared wary but crept toward it. Her ears, erect like radar detectors, sought feedback that might signal a threat. Again, she sniffed the air for any hint of danger.

"I'm going to call you Skinny. You certainly look the part."

I'm sure she had never smelled, much less eaten, a store-bought dog treat, and I wasn't sure how she would react to the hard, bone-shaped biscuits. I once mustered the courage to taste one. I found it almost tasteless, causing me to wonder why dogs loved them. Nevertheless, I hoped she would eat them. They contained large amounts of nutrients and calories ideal for this frail, pathetic looking dog.

She sniffed the treat then decided it was edible. Her tongue ensnared it. Without concern for the sand covering the morsel, she gobbled it up. In three loud crunches, it was gone.

"Hallelujah!" I yelled through clinched teeth, for fear I might frighten her away.

She looked in my direction. Her ears pointed skyward as she narrowed her eyelids to a squint.

Oh God. I hope I don't scare her away! I don't want her to die of starvation today.

I felt elated when she stayed. Holding my breath, I waited to see if she would search for the other treats. It took a few seconds before she found and dispatched another treat as she headed for the third. A nearby stray dog barked, at what I don't know, but the bark caused Skinny to rush to the next treat. She looked from side-to-side for danger, and seeing none, she gave the treat one crunch and swallowed it.

I watched as she walked to within three inches of another treat. Just then, a car sped into the dump, and the driver slammed on his brakes. The car stopped abruptly, raising a cloud of dust.

Frightened, Skinny tucked her tail, ran in front of my car, crossed the road, and dashed into the bushes where I had seen her seek refuge days earlier.

Two men exited the car and opened their trunk. They removed several large trash bags and tossed them onto the pile. Through the translucent bags, I could read a red hotdog label and identify scraps of bread. The new garbage would make some dog very happy. I hoped it would be the young dog I had just fed.

Anticipating the frightened dog would return, I dropped four treats on the ground and drove away. Somehow, I knew I would see her again.

Several days later, I parked at the dump and waited to see which, if any, dogs came to scavenge. I was prepared to feed a few of the starving ones.

Ten minutes later, a wreck of a car missing all its glass, chugged into the dump. Children in the backseat tossed garbage-stuffed plastic grocery bags through the rear and side window openings. One bag, thrown by the smallest child, landed on the car's trunk. Another burst opened as it hit the ground, spilling a clump of dry looking tortillas.

The car then sped away, creating a cloud of dust

149

mixed with black exhaust. As the car reached a certain speed, the trash bag on the trunk fell onto the middle of the road, spilling its contents.

Almost on cue, several dogs attracted by the smell of fresh garbage, descended on the dump. Among them was Skinny whom I had fed days earlier. She and a larger, better nourished male dog wrestled over the tortillas. One broke into several smaller pieces attracting five other dogs. A battle erupted.

Since Skinny was no match for the larger dogs, she retreated to the edge of the dump with a piece of tortilla hanging from her mouth. Apparently feeling safe there, she ate her find then waited for an opportunity to resume scavenging.

One of the bags of trash had rolled a short distance from the main heap. Skinny explored the errant bag as the pack rummaged among the more pungent bundles. She found something of interest, which she chewed and then swallowed. I hoped the item wasn't a piece of plastic that smelled of edible fare but contained nothing more than the potential to clog her intestines.

Finding nothing more in the isolated bag, Skinny turned to the newly scattered trash. She nosed around the edge of the pile then moved into its middle. Her search was interrupted by a larger dog who claimed the heap for himself. He bared his fangs, growled, ruffled his back hair, and arched his spine. Lunging at interlopers, he snapped his teeth as if to say, 'This is my trash. Stay away.'

Skinny returned to her bag and re-explored its contents. She removed a plastic wrapper, covered with red print, and then scampered across the road where she entered the bushes with the treasured item hanging from her mouth.

I walked to the small, cave-like entrance to the

bushes and dropped several treats, hoping Skinny would find them. I returned to my car and waited to see if she would come out for the treats. About to relinquish my vigil, I watched as Skinny crept from under the bushes then explored the treats. She gobbled them up, and with the last one in her teeth, she retreated to the bushes.

I drove away knowing that one less dog would starve to death that day.

Winter had arrived in Yucatan. This meant there were fewer people at the beach to leave food scraps for stray animals, and drinking water would be even harder to come by. Little rain fell during the winter. This meant no rain puddles. While temperatures had moderated they could still reach the mid-eighties. This was not a good time for stray dogs.

I purchased a plastic washbasin and took it to the dump area. I left it beside the path leading to the bushes where strays often took refuge from the sun, heat, and other dogs. Every few days, I filled it with water and hoped Skinny would be one of the dogs to benefit from it.

At times, I would fill the basin then sit in my car and wait to see if thirsty dogs found the water. Skinny was often among them. On those occasions, I dropped dog biscuits beside the pavement and left, hoping she would eat them.

This activity became an almost daily ritual. I was pleased to see strays, such as Skinny, eat and drink. I was most happy watching her gain weight, but I began to wonder if she had found another source of food besides mine.

Days passed into weeks and Skinny attained normal weight. I allowed myself to think she might grow up to be a healthy dog.

Over time, she recognized my car and associated

it with food. On each visit, I waited no more than a few minutes until she peeped from beneath the bushes then crept along the path toward the food I left at the side of the road.

If I got closer than twenty feet, she would run away. Knowing this, I dropped some treats then moved away, allowing her to eat stress free.

While she ate, I scanned her body, noting changes in her growth. Often, I spotted a new wound—no doubt the result of a fight over food scraps, but overall, she had done well.

With my vet's permission, and her provision of anti-parasite medication, I fed Skinny a wiener containing the pills, hoping to cure her of parasites that she and most dogs harbored.

I had no way of knowing Skinny's age, but I guessed she had been about four to six months old when I first saw her three months earlier. If so, it was time to have her spayed. However, I didn't know how I would capture her or transport her to a vet.

Neither the vet nor anyone I asked had a dog snare, and there were no dog pounds or dog catchers in the area who might loan me one.

With necessity being the mother of invention, I decided to make a snare. I purchased a long-handled broom, eye-hooks and nylon rope. With the removal of the straw portion of the broom and some engineering, I made a retrieval device.

With the help of my caretaker, Hugo, I would attempt to capture Skinny.

I took the snare from the trunk of my car and went to the bush-path where I dropped a treat. Within a minute, Skinny approached the treat, looked at me and the snare, and tucked her tail.

Does she think the stick is for beating her?

After a moment of standing still to assure her I

and the pole were no threat, she crept closer to the treat. With one swoop of her tongue, she snatched a treat and ran into the bushes.

Well this is not going to work.

"Hugo," I called, "bring some treats will you?"

While Hugo went to the car for the treats, I widened the snaring loop of the nylon rope to a diameter of two feet then spread it on the ground where I planned to place the treats. I laid the broom handle on the ground and pulled the slack rope against the pole. The snare and I were ready.

"What do you want me to do with these treats?" Hugo asked.

"Drop a few inside the loop," I said then kneeled beside the gripping end of the handle. "I hope she'll eat them and not notice the rope." I looked at Hugo. "When she's eating, I'm going to pull the rope and tighten the loop around her neck. Better put on your work gloves. You may have to grapple with her once she's snared."

"Give me a minute to get 'em on. They're dry and stiff."

Hugo placed the treats inside the loop then got his work gloves from his pants pocket. Like the gloves in the O.J. Simpson's trial, they were difficult to get on, but soon, they and Hugo were in place—a few feet behind me.

I had knelt four feet from the snare's loop. That might have been too close, but I had no choice given the length of the broom handle.

I waited and waited for Skinny to return. My knees began to ache. As the ache grew, I was ready to leave, but Skinny stuck her head outside the bushes. She sniffed the air and then approached the food lying inside the snare.

"Keep coming, girl. Keep coming," I whispered.

Skinny sniffed the air, looked left and right, then

153

tucked her tail and scampered away. Why? I do not
know.

"This ain't gonna work," Hugo said.

"I agree. We need something longer. Let's get
out of here. I need to consider other options. Besides,
it's getting hot out here."

"I have an idea," Hugo said, waving his hands as
we walked to the car. "Since we can't find a longer
pole, let's get another broom and join it with this
pole."

"Okay, but how are we going to join them?"

"Don't worry. I have a plan."

As we drove away, I glanced at the dog path via
my rearview mirror. Skinny scampered from the
bushes and ate the treats left on the ground.

The next morning, Hugo knocked on my kitchen
door. "I have the new snare," he said, waving the
eight-foot-long pole in the air.

One end of two broom handles had been pushed
into a tightly fitting twelve-inch-long piece of PVC
pipe. It was held in place by screws, making one long,
spliced pole.

"Do you think that will hold?" I asked, pointing
at the plastic sleeve covering the juncture of the poles.

"We'll just have to try . . . see what happens."

I drove to the dump with Hugo and parked in my
usual spot. No sooner had I turned off the engine than
a dump-assistant, looking ninety years old, came to
my door expecting garbage and a tip. His black baseball cap had a ripped top which flapped in the breeze.
His white shirt sleeves were tattered and covered with
dirty grease stains. The knees of his faded slacks had
several rips.

"Need help with your *basura*?" he asked,

pointing toward the trunk.

"No," I replied, "we're here to catch a dog."

"Take 'em all," he said, waving his arms. "They make a mess of the place. I no sooner clean it up than they scatter it again. Look at the mess they made last night."

I scanned the space, noticing that almost every bag of garbage had been ripped open and its contents

scattered.

"I'm not here to take all of them. We want the young, female dog with the brown and black spots on a white coat."

"Have you seen her this morning?" Hugo asked.

"Think I know the one you're talking about," the man said. "I ran her and her pack off this morning. They ran into the bushes across the road."

"Well, Hugo, we know she's in the neighborhood."

We made our way to the feeding spot on the path leading into the bushes. I placed the grafted poles on the ground then spread the snare rope into a large loop around some treats.

"Hugo, the washbasin is empty. Will you fill it, please?"

"Did you put water in the trunk?"

"Yes, it and your gloves are in the trunk."

Hugo filled the washbasin, nestled in the bushes fifteen feet away, then donned his gloves.

"Stand back," I said, kneeling on the sand.

"Let's see if she'll come out."

A few minutes later, I said, "I can't take this kneeling any longer. My knees are killing me, and it's getting hot. Let's take a break. We can wait in the car."

"Are you going to leave the treats?" Hugo asked.

"Yeah . . . leave one—no more, and leave the

snare. It'll be okay."

It felt good to stand and give my knees a break. The car air conditioning felt even better.

Ten minutes later, a pack of dogs trotted along the road toward us. My heart sank as I envisioned the pack taking up residence and scaring Skinny away. Worse yet, I did not want to proceed with the capture and have the pack smell the treats and perhaps fight for them—possibly injuring Skinny.

Hugo and I watched the approaching dogs. Their thirsty tongues dangled from panting mouths. Each dog carried its tail high above its back, like an African Meerkat on a hunt. The lead dog headed for the center of the trash heap where the dogs scavenged out of sight of the attendant.

"Let's hope all this rummaging doesn't scare Skinny," I said.

"Why don't we chase this pack out of here?" Hugo asked.

"How?"

"Blow the horn a few times. If that doesn't scare 'em off maybe the attendant will."

I tooted the horn, but the dogs paid no attention. However, the attendant did. He scampered out of his shack and walked toward the car, rubbing his eyes as if he had been asleep. He must have thought we were customers needing assistance.

Hugo lowered his window then pointed toward the dogs. "Yer dogs are back," he yelled.

"Damn it," the attendant shouted, running and waving his arms, while screaming obscenities at anything that moved.

Hugo and I laughed as the arm-flailing attendant pursued the dogs. They scattered in all directions. Within seconds, the dogs had vacated the dump, re-gathered on the road, and trotted west.

Despite our closed windows, we could hear salsa

music approaching us from the west. Within seconds, a dilapidated old car passed carrying several young guys who hung out its windows, waving local soccer team banners. Speeding east, toward Chelem, the driver blew his horn. The dog pack moved to the shoulder and then chased the speeding car.

"Glad they're gone," I said, "but I hope all the racket hasn't driven Skinny deeper into the bushes."

We waited for Skinny to make her appearance for what seemed like an eternity. As my patience wore thin, I asked, "Think anything is going to happen?"

"Give her a little more time," Hugo said.

"Okay. Twenty minutes. If she doesn't show up by then, we'll leave."

I started my stopwatch and waited. There were no passing cars, no trains of bicyclists, no jitney buses, no pedestrians. Nothing.

"God, this waiting is boring," I said. "Where is everybody?"

"I don't know, but it sure is quiet."

Twenty minutes passed and still, no Skinny.

"Time's up," I said. "Let's get out of here."

As I started the car, I noted a snout sticking out of the bushes.

"It's her!" I said.

"Yep," Hugo mumbled.

"Look, she's heading for the treat. Come on doggie. Come on. Get it."

Skinny took the treat, looked at us, and then walked back into the bushes.

"Come on, Hugo, let's go get her."

I placed a few treats inside the undisturbed loop of rope lying on the sand, knelt beside the pole, and waited for Skinny's return. Within minutes, she peeked from beneath the bushes then walked toward us.

"Come on, girl," I said, under my breath.

Staring at me, Skinny headed for the nearest treat. In doing so, she placed her left front foot inside the loop, but she did not take the treat.

"Oh no," I whispered, not wanting to snare just one leg. I wanted her head inside the loop, so I waited until she ate a treat.

"Hugo," I whispered, "get ready. On the count of three, I'm going to pull the rope."

"I'm ready," Hugo said.

"One . . . two . . . three," I whispered then yanked the loose end of the rope. The loop cinched around Skinny's neck. "I got her!"

She yelped, jumped, and lunged toward her home, almost pulling the pole from my hands. I held onto the gyrating broom handles with a death grip. The dog's end of the pole jerked about like a conductor's baton directing the 1812 Overture.

"Hugo, hold her," I yelled.

Skinny jumped up and down, whined, and pawed at the rope around her neck. She fell and then rolled on the ground, hurling sand in all directions.

Hugo rushed toward her, but he tripped and fell.

Skinny got to her feet and scampered beyond Hugo's reach.

"Get her!" I yelled.

"I'm trying!" Hugo yelled as he righted himself.

I don't know where Skinny's energy came from, but she suddenly had the strength of an ox. She squirmed then jumped two feet into the air. I heard a loud pop and felt something break. The plastic pipe sleeve had broken along the line of screw holes, freeing the broom handles.

Skinny ran toward the bushes, dragging one broom handle by the loop of rope around her neck.

I needed to free her of the rope and pole, to prevent injuries. I lunged at the free end of the escaping broom handle. With my toe being the only contact with the pole, Skinny's forward motion pulled the rope free of the "eye" hooks along the handle and then her neck. She escaped into the bushes, unharmed.

I wiped sweat from my brow and spat sand, which had been thrown in my face during the tussle.

"Well that's a fine how-do-you-do," I said, glaring at Hugo. "Give my regards to the pole's *engineer*."

"Don't blame me," Hugo said, "I did the best I could with what I had."

I smiled then said, "Tell the *engineer* he's fired."

Hugo laughed.

We gathered the pieces of our snare and then drove home to lick our wounds.

Hope this incident doesn't frighten Skinny away forever.

Over the next few weeks, I watched for Skinny in and around the dump while I replenished water in the communal washbasin.

Late one afternoon, Hugo and I visited the area across from the dump as the sun dipped below the tree tops. Shadows covered the path to the bushes the dogs knew as home.

I scattered a few biscuits on the path and took a seat on the shadow-cooled sand beside the path. I squirmed my butt into the sand, creating a more comfortable seat.

After waiting a few minutes, three stray dogs peeked from beneath the bushes. Single file, they walked along the path toward the treats, resting twelve feet from where I sat. The lead dog looked at me and then nosedived into the pile of treats. He growled at the other dogs as they approached the biscuits. The leader ate a treat then moved to another.

I don't dare try to scare them away. They may attack me for trying to "steal" their food.

The accompanying dogs crept around the leader's flanks and took several treats. The lead dog, teeth bared, growled and lunged at the nearest dog then snatched the last biscuit and trotted away. The others followed, bellies empty.

After the dogs were out of sight, I dropped a replacement treat in the path. As I did, I noticed Skinny's head protruding from beneath the bushes.

I placed another biscuit on the path and then dropped more, in a line, toward the spot where I reclaimed my seat in the sand. Avoiding quick or threatening moves, I sat down, waiting for Skinny to come out on her own terms. Who knows what psychic trauma I had caused her with the snare?

Please, come out and eat.

Much to my delight, she made her way toward the first treat then ate it. She then approached the second treat and ate it. With her head close to the ground, she stared at me, showing the lower portions of the white of her eyes. Slowly, she raised her head until we stared eyeball-to-eyeball. Within moments, she ate another treat. I grew nervous because she was closer not only to a treat but to me—the closest ever.

Does she remember me as the guy with the snare? Does she hate me? She got closer. I took a deep breath. *God, I hope she isn't going to attack me!*

I held my breath as she moved closer and evaluated the situation. I imagined she questioned whether or not she should move toward the next treat?

My butt grew numb. I wanted to shift my position but dared not move for fear of frightening her.

Come on, I repeated to myself. *Eat them up. Don't leave them for another dog.*

A muffler-less car roared past. Skinny jumped half-a-step backward and tucked her tail. Torn between eating or running, hunger won out. She stared straight at me and walked toward the next treat then ate it. A few treats later, she stood three feet from me. She looked up as if to ask, 'Is there any more?'

I eased my right hand into my pocket and got a treat. Gripping one end of it with my thumb and fingertip, I slowly extended it toward her. The closer the treat got to her the more she backed away.

"Come on . . . Come on," I whispered.

Hunger drove her forward. Without warning, she lunged, mouth open. My heart raced, and my arm recoiled. I dropped the treat.

She bit me!

My semi-scream didn't deter the dog from finishing the treat.

"Whew!" I said, with a sigh of relief while examining my finger. "There's no blood."

After a few seconds, I wondered if I dare try that again? I knew Skinny hadn't tried to bite me; she simply wanted the treat.

"Going to try that again?" Hugo asked.

I ignored the question as I tried to forget the numbness in my butt. I had to move or forever bury my dead butt in the hole where it rested. I inched my body into a semi-upright position and felt blood flow through my rear and legs. The numbness gave way to an ache.

How else can I do this feeding thing?

Getting another treat from my pocket, I said, "Hugo, I'm going to try again, but this time I'm going to be on my feet—in case I have to run."

Skinny stood her ground, staring at me then the treat.

I got myself into a squatting position then held as little of the treat as possible between my forefinger and thumb. I extended my at-risk digits toward her, hoping to avoid being bitten on her next attempt to be handfed.

From the intensity of her stare and the drop of her jaw, I knew she wanted the treat.

"Okay, come get it," I said, "but leave my fingers alone."

Skinny inched her nose toward the treat as I lowered my hand to the height of her head. She leaned forward to take the treat but hesitated for the longest time.

Fatigue, and maybe fear, caused my arm and hand to shake. *Easy... does... it.*

Skinny took one step forward, stretched her body and extended her head.

"Don't be afraid," I said. "Come on, girl. Take it."

Suddenly, I saw a blur and heard a crunch. I squeezed my eyelids closed and waited for God knows what—maybe pain, perhaps blood, maybe a missing arm, a severed digit or two, but I felt nothing. I opened my eyes, like a child awakening from deep sleep then focused on my out-stretched hand. Mercifully, Skinny had taken the treat—free of body parts.

Anxiety fleeing my body, my heart rate slowed, and I dropped my arm. I slumped, then relaxed so much my right hand opened, and the remaining treats fell to the ground. The smell and sight of the food was too much for Skinny to ignore—despite the fact they were an inch from my hand. To my surprise, she ate the treats as if I had not been there. I stretched my hand to stroke her head, but as I did, she dropped the last morsel from her mouth, tucked her tail, and jumped two feet backwards, ready to run.

"Oh God," I said, looking at Hugo. "She's frightened by touch. Guess I'd better not push my luck."

As I stood, Skinny moved farther away.

God, I hope she doesn't think I'm going to kick

or hit her.

I got a jug of water from the car then filled the plastic basin, which had, so far, not been stolen. Hugo and I returned to the car and waited. Within seconds, Skinny meandered to the basin and then almost emptied it. She stared at me, sniffed the air, then sauntered into the bushes.

Hugo refilled the water bowl then we drove away. I felt elated, knowing Skinny and I had become friends.

At home, I sat on the front porch, watching the waves lap the shore. I luxuriated in the cool, ocean breezes and enjoyed the company of my dogs, rescued months earlier. However, I couldn't help but think about the skinny stray at the dump. Something about her was compelling. I had to continue to help her, but I wasn't sure I wanted another dog, even if I could get her home. For the time being, I was content knowing she had food and water.

Skinny and I developed our own kind of relationship. Over time, she allowed me to get close, but I never petted her. For reasons unknown to me, she would not let herself be loved through human touch. I could only guess about possible past abuses by human beings.

One hot afternoon, I sat in my air-conditioned car and waited for her. After a few minutes, I grew weary of waiting and was about to drive away when she peeked from the bushes. She walked close to the car, sat on her haunches, stared at me, and waited for a treat.

I got out of the car and sat on the sand, waiting for her to approach me. In her cautious fashion, she meandered closer and took a treat from my extended hand. This time, however, I noticed something differ-

163

ent about her. She had a larger belly.

"Oh my god," I said. "Skinny, you're pregnant. Wow, girl, you're going to need a lot of food now."

She took two treats in her bite and waddled eight feet away. I watched as she stretched out on the sand to eat.

In the past, she had always stood to eat, but now she lay close by. I felt a warm sense of accomplishment. She trusted me. Our comfort bond was growing, causing me to want to reach out and pet her, but I did not.

Give her time, I thought. *Give her time.*

I started to sweat. The sea breeze had begun to die down, and I didn't like sitting under the hot sun without the cooling winds from the Gulf.

"Okay, little dog, I've had enough of this heat." I forced my aching knees to get me upright. "I'm going to leave a lot of food, and I'll fill your water bowl. Don't worry, I'll be back tomorrow."

I sat in my car for a minute, watching mother-to-be (MTB) enjoy her treats. Feeling some pride, I drove away.

On my visits to the dogs' bushy home, I would sit in the car until I saw MTB exit the bushes. After she made her appearance, I sat on the sand and hand feed her a few treats then dropped the remainder of the food onto the sand. I always placed the food near to my side, hoping she would come closer and let me pet her.

One afternoon, as I sat beside her, she stretched out on her belly. She ate treats and wagged her tail, creating a fan pattern in the sand. I leaned backwards, supporting myself on my outstretched arms. With my right hand, I stroked the tip of her tail. She jerked it away and looked back at me as if to say, 'Don't do that.' I was happy she did not run away.

"Okay, okay," I said. "I won't do that."

At the end of each visit, I filled the washbasin with water, but now, I added pediatric multivitamin as suggested by my vet. The drops contained calcium, iron, and minerals necessary for developing pups. I wanted MTB's unborn pups to have a good start for their life in the wild.

My visits became more and more enjoyable as MTB's belly grew larger and her teats became quite swollen. Their engorgement meant milk production was starting, and that signaled her delivery date was near.

Due to the size of her belly, her gait became more arduous, and she seemed to tire easily. To save her the effort of walking to the edge of the road where I had often fed her, I sat closer to her bushy home. I placed food on the sand and let her eat at her own pace.

One day, while feeding MTB, a roaring, mufflerless truck approached from the west and parked at the dump. The wreck of a vehicle had no cab, just the windshield, dashboard, steering wheel and a front seat filled by a rotund driver of advanced age and four children. There were no seatbelts.

The shabbily dressed children giggled, pointed toward MTB, and yelled, "Look, daddy, look. There's a dog! Let's take him home."

The driver tossed some trash on to the garbage heap while the children ran toward MTB.

One child's torn flip-flop strap made it difficult for him to walk. Nevertheless, he laughed as happily as if he had a million dollars.

"Don't get too close," I said. "If you do, she'll run away, and I want to finish feeding her."

The children stopped and muttered something in Spanish between pointing and giggling.

The driver approached me, nodded toward my car, and asked, "Having car trouble?"

"No. No trouble but thanks for asking."

"Is that your dog?" he asked.

"Kinda."

"Okay," the stranger said, "otherwise the kids would like to have him."

For what? To eat it? "It's a female, and she is *very* pregnant."

"Oh!" the driver said. I don't want no pregnant dog. They're too much trouble—too many mouths to feed."

Skinny stopped eating, raised her head, and surveyed the strangers. Surprisingly, she did not run away or growl at the intruders to deter the possibility someone might take her food.

"Well, gotta go," The elderly man said. "Good luck with your dog."

The group returned to the truck. The driver turned the ignition switch and the vehicle backfired two times before it moved forward. The children waved and yelled goodbye as they headed east.

"Skinny, you had better be glad you're pregnant, or you might have ended up with those kids."

It was noontime Saturday, and I had to go to the airport to pick up friends, Harold and Louise. They were celebrating Harold's completion of therapy for prostate cancer, which had caused his premature retirement.

Louise had always been a stay at home wife, despite having a law degree.

The United flight was on time, and my guests had no problems with luggage or customs. We were soon on the way to the beach.

We discussed the weather, health of some mutual friends, and a social event that we would be attending Wednesday night.

"There's news at the beach," I said. "I have a new dog. Well kinda, and I'm going to be a daddy."

"What are you talking about?" Harold asked.

"I've adopted another dog, but she doesn't stay at the house."

"Is she a sponsored shelter dog?" Louise asked.

"No, not a shelter," I said, "Her name was Skinny, but I now call her MTB. She lives in the bushes near the dump."

"Where," Louise asked. "and what does MTB mean?"

"MTB means Mother-To-Be. She's a dog I noticed rummaging through the dump a few months ago. She was almost dead from starvation, and as you know, I can't stand to see a dog suffer. I started leaving food for her, and over time, we've become friends—even though she won't let me pet her. She's 'great with child,' and I expect her to deliver any day now. If you don't mind, I want to feed her on our way to the house."

"Fine with me," Harold said.

"Great," Louise said, leaning over the front seat. "I'd like to see this MTB."

"Damn," I said, glancing toward the west. "It's going to rain. Ut oh. There are a few drops on the windshield."

"Yeah, look at those clouds," Harold said, "they look threatening. Glad we didn't have to fly through that."

"Wouldn't you know it," Louise said. "Our first day of vacation and it's going to rain."

"Don't worry," I said. "It may rain here but not at the beach. I'm sure we'll out run the storm."

Like small rocks, large drops of rain hit the windshield. A minute later, there was a downpour, obscuring sight of the road. I slowed the car to a crawl and turned on the wipers, headlights, and emergency flashers.

"Ever have tornados here?" Louise asked.

"Never heard of any," I said.

"Harold, watch for funnel clouds...especially behind us," Louise said, anxiety coloring her words. "Those clouds are black—ominous looking."

"Think there is anything to worry about?" Harold asked.

"I don't think so. This should be over soon, and then we'll be on our way."

Within minutes, the storm moved north toward the Gulf, and we resumed our trip northward. We splashed through pot holes and puddles, almost drowning the car.

Along the way, I pointed out a temporary bull-ring constructed of tall sticks covered with multi-colored oilcloths in varying states of wholeness. Several fluttered in the wind like a boat's untethered sail.

"Those oilcloths are used to prevent outsiders from seeing the bullfights for free," I said.

"Don't tell me they have bullfights there," Louise said, rubbing condensation from her window to better see the rickety structure.

"Yep, one every night for a week," I said.

"I want nothing to do with bullfighting," Louise said, shaking her finger.

"Bullfights in the villages are pretty awful," I said, "but if you want to experience local color, we can go."

At the dump, I parked on the north shoulder of the road. Paper darted about as a strong land breeze blew over the area. The sky was clear and sunny except to the south.

A huge pile of trash filled the dump, standing

twenty feet tall. It must have been there for days. The vile stench of rot seeped into the car, stinging our nostrils. We were reluctant to take a deep breath.

"God, that trash stinks," Louise said.

"Yeah, and it looks like that storm is following us," I said, looking over my shoulder.

"From the way those clouds are moving, the storm should be here in fifteen minutes," Louise said.

"We'll see. When I stop to feed MTB, I usually sit in the car until she shows up." I pointed to my right. "See those bushes. She lives somewhere under that mass of vegetation."

We waited for MTB to make her appearance while we discussed inconsequential things as the acrid stench from the dump encased the car.

"I don't think your dog is coming," Louise said, shaking her head.

"It does seem she's taking longer than usual," I said. "Maybe I should sit in the sand as I usually do."

Wrinkling his brow, Harold asked, "Didn't you say she was about ready to deliver?"

"Yes . . . and I'm wondering if she has delivered and won't leave her pups. I'm tempted to crawl under those bushes and see what I can find."

"Have you *ever* crawled under there?" Louise asked.

"No, but I've never had reason to."

The bushes are called "prickly leaf" by the locals. Their dense foliage looked like a giant head of broccoli. Each bush has a large, central trunk and numerous long, fragile side branches. Its leaves resembled maple leaves and overlapped each other, screening the ground from sunlight and rain. Each leaf had thousands of tiny, rigid thorns that were easily dislodged and could penetrate the skin, leaving a stinging sensation that lasts for hours.

I looked at Harold. "I have an old towel in the trunk. I'm going to use it to cover my hand, so I can break off a few of those branches to make an opening. I want to have a look inside."

"Do you have to look *now*?" Louise asked, the tone of her voice questioning my sanity.

"No, but I'm curious."

"Louise is right," Harold said. "You don't know what you'll find in there . . . maybe wild dogs, the Boston strangler, or something worse."

"I know, but MTB may have delivered and needs food or water . . . Besides, I'm anxious to see her pups."

"You do what you have to," Louise said, "but I'm not getting out of this car. Breathing the full stench of that dump would kill me. Besides, it's hot outside."

"I think I'll give it a try," I said, getting out of the car. "Wish me luck."

"I'll stand guard," Harold said, getting out of the car, "in case a herd of wild boar, or whatever, goes in after you."

I got the towel from the trunk and wrapped it around my right hand, leaving some wiggle room for my thumb.

At the bushes, I got down on-all-fours. The dry, warm sand grated against my unprotected hand and knees.

Wish I hadn't worn shorts.

I broke off several branches in the area of the well-trodden path that led into the bushy domain. I took care not to let the thorny leaves touch my skin. Within seconds, I had enlarged the opening enough to get inside. I stuck my head into the shade of the bush where the temperature was ten degrees cooler. I allowed a few moments for my eyes to dark adapt. Soon, I could see across the shady area.

"Wow," I said, "It's like a gothic cathedral in here."

"What do you mean?" Harold asked, from his post at the "cathedral door."

"Well, most of the lower branches are broken off . . . maybe fallen off. I can stand up in here . . . interesting . . . The upper branches remind me of the arches you see on the ceiling of gothic churches." I looked around for a few seconds. "There're no green leaves in here. They're all at the outer edges of the bush." Suddenly, a gust of wind blew overhead. "Wow! When the wind blows, the leaves part and light streams in like you see in paintings of old Dutch churches."

"Got any matches to light a prayer candle?" Harold asked through a chuckle.

"What do you see in there?" Louise yelled, presumably from an open window?

"So far, I see nothing but trash and dead tree limbs and leaves," I yelled. "I'm going in a little farther."

Hunkered over, I stepped over the debris left by nature and stray dogs. Here and there were scraps of rags, bones of God knows what, weathered paper, plastic shopping bags, a rusty motor-oil can, and an occasional beer can.

I rounded the main trunk of the bush, using my towel-wrapped hand to break off minor limbs and twigs obstructing my path. Sweat dripped from my brow, and whiffs of dump-stench raked my nostrils.

A clap of thunder caused me to think the storm had moved closer to the dump. Gusts of wind rattled the leafy lattice of the dome allowing shifting shafts of light to pepper the cathedral floor. The smell of rotting garbage was as noxious inside the bushes as at the dump, causing me to breathe through my mouth to avoid the stench. I swatted at biting flies, but there

171

was no sign of MTB.

"Harold," I called out, "she isn't under this bush. I'm going in a little deeper."

"Hurry," Harold yelled. "I think it's going to rain soon."

The cathedral grew darker the deeper I moved into the space. The approaching storm and darkening sky didn't help visibility. Holding onto the main trunk of another bush, I swung to its opposite side, just as a gust of wind opened a skylight in the cathedral dome.

"Oh my God!" I yelled, falling to my knees.

"Are you all right?" Harold called.

"Oh, MTB!" I yelled.

"What the hell is going on in there?" Harold yelled. "Is everything OK?"

My sight became distorted by a flood of tears. So overcome with emotion, I could not speak. I had found her.

MTB lay in a shallow hole she had dug in the leaf-strewn dirty sand for her deliveries. Her extended body rested on dirty scraps of rags she had scavenged to cradle her new born puppies when they arrive, but. her abdomen was bloated, and her legs were extended like steel rebar in uncompleted concrete columns at a construction site.

Hanging from her birth canal was a half-deliver-ed puppy, still encased in its dried delivery sac. The dead puppy's head lay against the dirty rags, soaked and surrounded by a pool of dried brown blood. MTB's mouth had gaped open to allow another pool of blood to spill onto the dirt. The now dried blood had the uncanny shape of a hallo around her head. Cuddled at her belly were five puppies, which, like their mother, were dead and covered with buzzing flies.

I wept and pounded the earth as though it was the culprit. I felt as if my heart had been ripped out, leaving me breathless.

Concerned by my silence, Harold rushed to my side.

"Oh, no," he said, wrapping his arm around my shoulder while staring at the carnage.

Thunder rumbled in the distance and the wind's force reached a temporary crescendo that rattled and opened the "roof."

Burdened with sorrow I hadn't known since my father's death, I rocked back and forth on my knees. I wanted to scream, but somehow, I couldn't. The scream was stuck in my throat.

"Somebody poisoned her," I sobbed. "They gave her rat poison."

Harold squeezed my shoulder and murmured, "We need to get out of here."

I couldn't bear to look, and yet, I couldn't look away.

Harold repeated his mandate, "We need to get out of here."

"I can't just leave her . . . I can't."

A loud clap of thunder rumbled overhead as a powerful gust of wind ravaged the leaves above our heads. A few leaves fell around me, joining the dead ones on the ground.

Harold put his hands in my armpits, tugged upward, and repeated, "We have to get out of here. We don't want to be in here in a lightning storm."

"I can't leave her."

The storm was now at the door steps of the cathedral. The leaves rustled overhead as the entire bush swayed back and forth in the gusting wind.

"Look at those . . . poor . . . pups," I said, pointing at the dead puppies.

"Wait a minute," Harold said, "Something moved."

"What are you talking about?" I asked, looking

up into his face.

"Look, one of the puppies is moving . . . It's moving!"

I wiped my tears and stared at the puppies cuddled in death. I blinked then blinked again. Was I seeing things? *Did something move?* I could have sworn one puppy moved a few millimeters. "Oh my God, one's alive," I yelled.

Disregarding health hazards, I thrust my hand into the mass of dead puppies, pushing them aside in an effort to identify the body we thought had moved. Bugs scampered as green flies fled the carcasses and hovered overhead. The stench of death so fouled the air, we tried not to breath.

The puppy's bodies felt cold and stiff. I pushed them apart, searching for the one puppy I prayed was still alive. The sorting process seemed to take hours. The pup we thought had moved was dead, but the weak movements of the pup beneath her led us to where we needed to go.

The live, limp pup breathed as if each breath would be her last. Her tongue curled in her open mouth as she attempted to cry but did not have the energy to utter a sound.

Located at the bottom of the heap, she had, no doubt, been the firstborn. Because of the puppy's position, MTB's hemorrhage had flowed over her. The dried brown blood was encrusted with trash and had created a glue-like bond between the surviving pup and a dead sibling. I moved the dead and live pup back and forth like a hinge, breaking the blood-bond that held them as captive as Siamese twins.

I cradled the blood-encrusted, live pup in the palm of my right hand. "Let's get her home," I said to Harold. "Let's see if we can get some water in her."

Harold preceded me, pushing branches and small limbs out of our path as we rushed toward the car.

"Harold," I asked as we neared the car, "will you drive? I'll direct you."

Harold got behind the steering wheel, and I sat on the passenger's seat.

"What are you guys doing?" Louise asked, peering over the front seat.

"Where are the keys?" Harold asked.

"Harold," I said, "the car is already running."

"God, I was so excited, I hadn't noticed."

"Gosh, that's one small pup," Louise said, "The poor thing doesn't look like it's doing too well. What is all that brown stuff?"

"Blood," I said. "MTB was poisoned. She hemorrhaged to death. This is the only survivor, and she's covered with her mother's blood."

"Oh my," Louise said, slumping back in her seat.

As Harold drove, I picked at the dried blood while stimulating the pup's back to promote her breathing. I got an old T-shirt from the glove box that I used for car cleaning then wrapped it around the puppy to help maintain her body temperature.

God, please spare this pup.

"There's the house on the right," I said to Harold, nodding toward the house. "Push the open button on the remote. It's on the sun visor."

The garage door opened too slowly for me, but finally, we drove inside. Louise scampered from the back seat then opened my door. I steadied my right hand and its precious package as I pushed myself from the car.

My rescued dogs came running, tails wagging. They must have smelled the blood and were anxious to know what I had. This time, I ignored their attention.

I went to the kitchen and placed the t-shirt-wrapped pup on the counter beside the sink. I adjusted the water to the body temperature of a healthy pup.

I removed the t-shirt and let a few drops of water flow over the puppy. She didn't appear to object as the waste water turned dark reddish brown, dissolving the dried blood.

"Louise," I asked, "will you continue this? I'm going to see if I can find an eyedropper."

I had a bottle of liquid vitamins I had purchased for MTB's drinking water. The bottle had a plastic drop-per, which I removed and washed.

Racing to the kitchen, I yelled, "I found the eye-dropper!"

Louise had done a great job of removing the dried blood from the puppy now being dried.

"Thanks," I said, glancing at the pale pup while removing a drinking glass from a cabinet. I filled it with tepid tap water and dunked the tip of the dropper in the liquid. Squeezing the dropper's black rubber bulb, a few drops of water were sucked into the attached plastic cylinder.

After placing the puppy on her stomach, I lifted her head then eased my little finger into her mouth. This created a small opening through which I inserted the eyedropper. Pinching the bulb, I forced a few drops of water into her mouth. While waiting for the pup to swallow, I held my breath.

"Swallow little puppy," I whispered. "Please, swallow."

Nothing happened.

"Maybe I should give her a little more."
This time, I placed the end of the eyedropper deeper into the puppy's mouth. With one long squeeze on the bulb, water flowed into her mouth.

"She swallowed it!" I said. "She swallowed it."

Harold and Louise hugged each other.

"Thank God," Harold said and smiled.

I smiled as I experienced a sense of relief.

"Don't get too excited," Louise said, "You've got

to get a lot more water in her than that."

With a sense of invincibility, I refilled the eye-dropper then reinserted it in the pup's mouth. I squeezed the bulb and watched the water flow into her mouth. A few drops rolled out of her mouth, but a few were swallowed.

I'm getting good at this.

"I'm guessing her stomach is about the size of an acorn," I said, rubbing my itching nose with my wrist, "so I don't want to overload it, but I've got to get her to take a few more drops."

Once more, I positioned the filled dropper in the pup's mouth. I squeezed the bulb and waited for a reaction. She made a half-hearted attempt at swallowing, but most of the water rolled from her mouth.

"Maybe we've reached the limit of her strength to swallow," Louise said.

"You might be right," I said, "I'll give her a rest before I try again."

I turned the pup onto her side, thinking she might breathe better in that position. I tucked a towel around her to help retain her body heat then let her rest.

"How long do you think we should wait?" I asked Louise.

"I'd give her an hour of undisturbed rest," Louise replied, "but don't forget she may have hemorrhaged internally just like her mother."

"I don't want to think about that," I said, feeling frustrated and depressed. "How'd you like coffee or a drink while we wait?"

"I'll have a cup," Louise said.

"Me too," Harold said.

We washed our hands, and then I filled the coffee pot with water. Louise selected a strong Colombian grind and added it to the pot.

Waiting for coffee, we sat mute around the kitchen table and watched the resting puppy.

177

The coffee pot water boiled, hissed, and bubbled. After five minutes, the aroma of coffee filled the room.

"It's ready," I said, pouring a cup for each of us.

We didn't speak for a while as we drank our coffee.

After a few minutes, I asked Harold, "How's your new business adventure."

"It's going well," he whispered.

We kept our voices low as if we were afraid we might startle the pup. As we talked, I kept an eye on the clock. The minute hand crept from indicator line to indicator line. The loud "click, click" dominated the quietude. I felt more and more anxious. Squirming, pacing, and rapping the table, I waited for the hour to pass.

When the appointed hour arrived, I said, "Louise, would you try your hand at getting the pup to swallow some water?"

"Sure, but I don't know that I'd do any better than you, but . . . I'll give it my best."

Louise drew tepid water from the faucet then filled the dropper. Her hand moved with a fine tremor as she inserted the eyedropper then squeezed the bulb. We watched water flow into the puppy's mouth.

I guessed half the water in the eyedropper had been swallowed.

"That swallowing attempt seemed weaker than previous ones," Harold said.

"Damn," Louise said, frowning first at me and then Harold. "Let's give her fifteen minutes then try again."

"It's getting late," I said, "I'll continue with the water. Why don't you guys go to bed? I'm sure you're tired after traveling all day."

"Sounds good to me," Louise said, "I could use some sleep, but I don't want you staying up all night."

178

She headed for the bedroom then stopped, turned, and said, "How about I get two hours sleep then let you get two hours sleep. Maybe Harold can take a shift as well."

"Surely," Harold said.

My guests went to bed, and I began the vigil. I attempted to hydrate the pup, but her swallowing attempts grew weaker.

God, let this puppy hang on until morning so I can get her to the vet.

I made several more attempts but with diminishing results.

Before I knew it, two hours had passed, and Louise made her way to the kitchen, brushing sleep from her eyes.

"How's she doing?" Louise asked.

"Not well. She's swallowed very little water. Her swallowing attempts are quite feeble."

"Sorry to hear that," Louise said, rolling up the sleeves of her robe. "Why don't you get some sleep? I'll do what I can."

Despondent and aching inside, I went to bed. Four hours later, my alarm startled me awake. I was reluctant to go to the kitchen for fear of what I might find, but I had to make the trip.

As I walked into the kitchen, I saw Harold drinking a cup of coffee at the table. He stared at the ocean.

"Good morning," he said, glancing at me then turning back toward the Gulf. "We were so busy last night I forgot to look at the ocean. You're lucky. You get to see it every day." Harold faced me. "Want some coffee?"

"No, thanks but how's the puppy doing?"

"Not good. She took a few drops when I first started, but she's not swallowing anything now."

"She's going to die," I said, my voice breaking.

"It doesn't look good," Harold said, putting down

his coffee cup.

From the hallway came footsteps. Louise had joined us. "I couldn't sleep. How's the pup doing?"

With tears welling in my eyes, I said, "She's dying."

With lead feet, I walked to the counter and peeked under the t-shirt and looked at the pup.

Don't die . . . please don't die.

I watched her chest rise, pause, and then slowly fall. The respirations were labored, gasping in nature, with long pauses between breaths. These were agonal respirations. I knew the end was near. I now wept for MTB and her puppy.

Harold hugged me and patted me on the back. His stubby beard scratched my face. Louise joined him, engulfing me in their embrace.

The puppy's shallow breathing grew weaker then stopped. I covered her with a towel and wept—not just for the loss of the pup but the fact she never knew her mother nor she her pup.

Louise wiped a tear. "What now?"

"I'm not sure," I replied.

I walked outside to greet the rising sun. A flood of tears found their way to the surface. I shuddered with a wave of grief as I walked around the yard listening to the sounds of the waves. I trudged over the sand toward the shoreline and slumped onto the beach and cried as if to fill the ocean.

I sat alone for fifteen minutes as Louise's question reverberated in my mind.

Motionless, she and Harold stood on the front porch staring in my direction. I joined them. Each moved to one side of me and embraced me for a moment.

We walked into the kitchen where we sat down at the table.

As if to break the silence, Louise asked, "Coffee

anyone?"

After a few seconds, I said, "I have to bury her with MTB."

There was a brief silence.

"You can't go back there, Louise said. "Bury her here."

"No, I want to bury her with her mother." My voice choked with tears.

"Okay," I'll go with you," Harold said, "When do you want to go?"

"I'd like to go now, but first I want to get a tarp from the garage—"

"Tell me where it is," Harold said, "and I'll get it."

"To the right of the door, first shelf."

Louise and Harold left the kitchen saying, "We'll meet you at the car as soon as we get dressed."

For a few minutes, I just stood at the counter where I had watched the pup's life ebb away. With great deference, I picked her up, wrapped the t-shirt around her, then carried her to the car.

Harold sat at the steering wheel. "I'll drive," he said. "The tarp is in the trunk."

"Thanks," I said.

Sitting on the front seat, I cradled the shrouded puppy in my cupped hands.

Harold found his way to the dump and parked the car off the road. All was quiet except for the swooshing sound of air flowing from the dashboard vents.

"Okay . . . It's time," I said.

How I wish this wasn't necessary.

I stepped into the warming day as Harold got the tarp and shovel from the trunk.

"I'm going with you," Louise said.

"Louise, you'll not be comfortable in there," Harold said.

"Harold, this is something I *want* to do," she said,

cocking her head to the left and tightening her lips.

I led the cortege into the bushes, causing a scrawny dog to scamper from our path. We pushed deeper into the cathedral. The stifling stench of the dump and death hovered in the morning air.

Harold and Louise cupped a hand over their nose and mouth for protection from the acrid smell. We all swatted at insects determined to devour us.

Mother-To-Be and her pups were just as we had left them. I knelt on the dead leaves that surrounded her and placed the t-shirt-wrapped puppy next to her belly.

Flies seemed determined to drive us away as they buzzed around our heads. Harold and Louise waved their hands to deflect them from my face.

I used one end of the t-shirt to position the dead puppies side-by-side, so each puppy's head touched their mother's body. Since Mother-To-Be had dug a hole for her delivery bed, there was no need to dig another.

I placed the blue tarp over the bodies and tucked it under MTB and her pups. I dug a shovel of dirt and let the soil slide onto the tarp-covered bodies.

I still remember the sound of that dirt falling on the tarp, now a plastic shroud.

Louise emptied a shovel of sand onto the tarp and then passed the shovel to Harold who repeated the ritual. He handed the shove to me. I completed the burial, made the sign of the cross, and then prayed a prayer I had written for another dog several months earlier.

God,

Please admit these, your creations,
   through heaven's garden gates.
May they share in the glee of angels
   forever wagging their tails with joy.

Assign an angel to pat their heads and rub
    their bellies to their unending delight
May they never know pain, rejection,
    hunger, or thirst.
May they know your perpetual love as
    you cuddle them in your unending,
    loving embrace.
As they live forever in my memory, grant
    them eternal peace.
Amen.

"Amen," Harold and Louise said.

I had no assumptions that the tarp would prevent anything, but I couldn't bear the thought of throwing sand on their bare bodies or knowing scavengers and insects would treat either MTB or her pups like so much refuse even though nature's dissolution process had already begun.

There was little conversation between the three of us. Our thoughts were filled with loss.

Days passed into weeks and weeks into months.

Every time I pass the cathedral, I think of what I had lost, but deep down inside, I know other dogs in need of help and mothers-to-be will cross my path. My only hope is I can do more for the new ones than I had been able to do for M.T.B.

For now, I wait for fate to send me another challenge with a wagging tail.

It is shameful for our species that the dog is man's best friend when man is the worst friend of the dog.

Eduardo Lamazón

Chapter 7

Doggie in the Window

I dropped a handful of hard, pea-sized pellets of dog food in the steel bowl. It rang like an empty Buddhist's alms bowl. No sooner had the bowls been filled and my back turned, black birds swooped down from the roof and devoured my dogs' breakfast.

The birds ate more than my dogs. I had to find a way to put a stop to this high-flying larceny.

To date, my only remedy had been standing near the bowls and shooing the birds away as the dogs ate. Other times, I sat in the kitchen watching the bowls. If a bird approached, I would either yell or clap. In either case, the birds retreated and waited for an "all's clear" signal from a lookout bird. On its cue, the flock returned, continuing their feast on dog food.

Avian aggression had gotten to the point the dogs were afraid to eat while the black birds hovered nearby.

I pondered the situation and inquired of friends and villagers as to what I could do to rid myself of this black-winged plague. I received all kinds of advice, but none made sense.

Not only was the theft of dogfood becoming expensive, the birds would congregate along the edge of the swimming pool and drink. I wasn't concerned they would drink the pool dry. The problem had to do with their droppings that decorated the pool coping. The removal of their poop required a scouring every morning and evening. The birds had to go. Their presence had become a health and esthetics problem.

I had considered feeding them poison, but I was afraid the birds might drop some of it into the areas frequented by my, and other, dogs. If that happened, I could wind up with dead pets.

I resorted to the use of firecrackers as suggested by a friend. The concussion type seemed to work best, but the effect lasted about forty-eight hours—the time it took for the ringing in my ears to clear. Before long, the birds ignored the bang and compressive wave of the fire-crackers. They returned to dine minutes after a firecracker had exploded. I wasn't getting much "bang" for my buck.

Friday evenings, I often attended a social event at the English Language Library in Merida, the capital city of the state of Yucatan. Many tourists and expats attended these events. The library served as a kind of clearing house for solutions to all kinds of problems peculiar to new comers in Yucatan.

One Friday, I attended the event to query as many people as possible about a solution to my bird problem. I received all kinds of input, but none of the suggestions seemed worthy of excitement. Besides, I had tried many of the suggestions, and they hadn't worked.

That evening at the library event, I met a tall, fair skinned man with a heavy Spanish accent. His expensive linen suit reeked of cigarette smoke.

We discussed my bird problem.

"Shoot them," he said.

"Shoot them?" I asked, "Isn't it illegal to discharge firearms in this state?"

"*Si*, except for BB guns," the stranger said then grinned.

"While I'm fed up with the birds and their mess, I don't want to kill them . . . Well, most of the time I don't. I just want them gone."

Trying to reassure me, the stranger said, "*Señor*, don't worry so much. A BB will not *keel* the birds, but it will give them a strong *stinging* sensation and deter their return."

"A BB gun? Where can I get one? By the way, what is your name? In case I get arrested for firing a BB gun, I'll need you to bail me out of jail."

"*Mi nombre* is Bill Sexton," he said, extending his hand in greeting.

I was surprised to hear an English sounding name for someone who had so many Mayan features. He seemed aristocratic in demeanor, causing me to wonder about his knowledge of BB guns.

"Bill, you don't know how glad I am to meet you," I said, shaking his hand. "My name is Frank."

Bill smiled. "You should be able to buy a BB gun at any large toy store or in some of the larger department stores. As a matter of fact, I saw some BB guns in the sporting goods department of that large store on the north side of Merida . . . London's. Have a look there."

"I know that store, but I've never been in their sporting goods department. As a matter of fact, I didn't know they had one. I'll check it out . . . as a matter of fact, I'll go tomorrow. Thank you so much for you input."

"My pleasure and good luck."

"May I buy you a drink . . . as a thank you gift?"

"Make it a Chardonnay."

Saturday morning, I stood at the entrance to London's department store, waiting for the store to open. The large marble façade provided shade from the morning sun and its heat.

Inside, I could hear the opening bell ring. A guard walked to the door and unlocked it.

I made a bee-line for the escalator to the second floor where I encountered a customer service clerk. Her name tag read Maria. "Maria, can you please direct me to the sporting good department?"

"*Si señor.* I would be happy to escort you. Please, follow me."

Maria was Mayan and short in stature. She wore high heeled, platform shoes, no doubt to make her appear taller. Her formal looking dark blue suit contrasted with a starched white shirt that smelled of cologne being sprayed on customers passing the first-floor cosmetics department.

We wound our way through a maze of displays arranged as though the store manager didn't want customers to find the sporting goods department.

Once in the sporting goods area, Maria introduced me to the department manager and then said, "Would you please help this gentleman?"

"Si," the manager said in an officious way. "How may I help you?"

"Well, I need a BB gun. Do you have any?"

"Yes, right this way, *señor.*"

We walked among the fishing rods, tents, and hiking boots toward the back of the department. There, on the wall were several racks of shiny rifles, shot guns, and BB guns—locked behind glass doors.

The clerk removed a large ring of keys from his belt and set about unlocking the doors then the pad-lock and chain threaded through the rifles trigger guards.

He handed me the nearest BB gun. It was a fierce looking rifle with a bright gun-metal-blue barrel and an carved walnut stock depicting bears and a deer being chased by hunt dogs.

This is quite fancy for a BB gun.

"What do you thing about this one?" the clerk asked.

Looking at the carvings on the stock, I jokingly asked, "Have many bears in Yucatan?"

The clerk didn't smile. I guess he didn't find my remark humorous.

"It's a hand-lever-action shooter," he said, moving the lever to the cocked position in less than a second. He aimed at the ceiling and pulled the trigger.

I was afraid he had shot the light at which he aimed the gun, but I heard nothing but an anemic 'click.'

"BBs are loaded here," the manager said, pointing to a swing-away cover for a small-bore tube beneath the barrel. "This tube holds one hundred fifty BBs."

"Wow," I said, holding the rifle to my shoulder and peering through the sight. "I can't believe this is a BB gun. It looks like the kind of rifle that might be used by a soldier. May I try the lever action?"

"*Si, Señor.* The gun isn't loaded . . . go ahead. Try it."

"You're sure it isn't loaded?"

"Very sure, *Señor.*"

I pulled the action lever down until I heard a click. It moved like a well-engineered machine. The gun was cocked and ready to fire. I raised it to my shoulder, aimed through the professional looking site, and then squeezed the trigger. The gun made a popping sound with an almost imperceptible recoil against my shoulder.

"I can't believe this is a BB gun."

"I assure you, *señor*, it's nothing more than a BB gun . . . a very *good* BB gun. Would you like to see the other gun? It's cheaper than the one you're holding."

"How much cheaper?"

Looking at the price tag of the racked gun, the clerk said, "This one is 200 *Pesos* cheaper."

"That's $20.00 less than this gun, and this one's so much better looking than that one." I turned the costlier rifle over in my hand. "No, I think I'll take this one . . . It's beautiful."

"Alright, *señor*, please step this way, and I will write up the bill."

I signed the charge slip, while the clerk placed the gun into a green plastic bag, shaped like a rifle case.

I thanked the manager and turned to leave when the clerk asked, "Do have BBs?"

"Oh, my gosh! I don't. Thanks for asking. I need some."

"No problem, *señor*. I'll get them."

The clerk returned with BBs and the sale was completed. I added the box of BBs to the rifle bag and left the department happy. *Now, I have the answer to my bird problem.*

I had some free time and decided to explore the store's second floor. I strolled along aisles to the far end of the floor where I found the candy department.

There were barrels after barrels and jars after jars containing all kinds of candy—a diabetic's delight or nightmare, depending on one's point of view or diagnosis. Everything looked so inviting, I wanted to fill several candy bags with a variety of chocolate goodies then devour them on my way out of the store.

I explored each candy cabinet and read every label. When I came to the end of the last display case, I walked behind it to see if there was more candy.

Sure enough, there was, but to my surprise, there was something more wonderful. I had found the entrance to the pet department.

I didn't know London's sold pets.

I forgot about candy and stepped through the wide doorway into the well-lighted, welcoming pet department. The floor shined like glass, and the air was heavy with the smell of pet sanitizer. On the right side of the room was a wall of aquariums of varying sizes. Many were filled with exotic, tropical fish. The wall on the left side of the room was lined with bird cages which held Yucatecan birds as well as some endangered African parrots.

The walls on either side of the entrance displayed dog collars, leashes, and pet clothing. The wall opposite the entrance was constructed of clear glass behind which stood three rows of stacked shiny, stainless steel cages to house dogs and cats.

There were several breeds of cats but only one dog. Much to my delight, it was a chestnut-colored miniature Dachshund—my favorite breed. In the past, I had owned three and now I have one, Greta, back in the U.S. She was seventeen years old.

As I approached the glass wall, a tall clerk, dressed in a white lab coat, stepped from behind a closed door and greeted me.

"*Buenos dias*," he said in English. "Do you like dachshunds?"

"Very much; I've owned several over the years and love them."

I moved closer to the glass wall to better see the only dog on display. On the lower right side of the dachshund cage was an information card written in Spanish.

Breed: Dachshund   **Whelped**: 01-09-07
      Miniature
Color: Brown/Red   **Immunization:** 03-10-07
Sex: Female
Price: 16,000 Pesos [$1,600 US]
Visitors: 03-12-07   **Certification**: Yes

The female puppy seemed happy to see me (or was it the clerk). She tried to climb up and out of the cage, wagging her tail fast enough to create a breeze that sent wood shavings, covering her cage floor, flying. Even though her cage was behind a glass wall, I could hear her whine of excitement.

"Would you like to hold her?" the clerk asked.

"Yes . . . very much," I said then smiled.

I wondered, could it be that the puppy hadn't been out of that cage since March 12, 2007.

The salesman left the main room, and seconds later, he appeared behind the cages where he opened the door of the dachshund's prison. The puppy licked his hand as he removed her from the cage. The clerk closed the cage door then disappeared from view.

Seconds later, he reentered the room where I waited. Under the protective cover of his left hand, he carried the squirming puppy in his right hand and held her against his chest. He motioned for me to take her.

I leaned my gun case against the wall and clutched the puppy to my chest. She began licking my chin and neck.

"My, she's a squirmer," I said.

"She's very excited and happy to see her new *padre*," the clerk said then smiled.

Is this clerk being sincere or making a sales pitch he thinks I can't resist.

The puppy smelled very perfumy—like jasmine.

"Did you spray her with perfume?" I asked.

194

"She was sprayed with a dog-coat *freshener*."

"You were *very* generous with it."

"Don't worry. It's *not* toxic and wears off quickly."

"That card on the front of her cage . . . What does the entry *Visits* mean?"

"That's the last date the dog was handled by a client."

That card reads March 12, 07, and it's now May 15th. This poor puppy hasn't had any human contact for over two months. That's horrible! "May I put her on the floor?"

"Certainly, *señor*."

"What if she makes a *mistake?*"

"It won't be problem. By all means, put her on the floor if you like."

I placed the puppy on the shiny vinyl floor. She sniffed my shoes then tried to jump up on my leg but was unable to maintain her footing on the slippery floor. She fell at my feet. Repeated attempts to jump on my leg were rewarded with repeated falls to the floor. Nevertheless, her tail never stopped wagging.

"Let's not keep doing that little puppy," I said. "I'm afraid you'll hurt yourself."

The clerk dropped a small piece of dry dog food on the floor. The puppy must have liked its smell because she scampered across the floor to get it.

Her little paws were unable to hold her upright on the polished vinyl. Several times, she slipped and found herself spread-eagle. At other times, she landed on her rump or on her side. Nevertheless, she continued trying to cross the slick floor in pursuit of additional bits of a treat.

I wondered if her eagerness for a treat might be an indication of hunger.

"Let's give her an *"A"* for effort," I said then smiled.

195

"She is persistent, isn't she?" the clerk said.

The only exercise this poor dog is going to get is picking herself up from this slick floor, and that isn't good. "She's having too much trouble trying to walk on this floor," I said. "Would it be okay if I took her onto the carpeted area of the candy department?"

"I'm sorry, *señor*, but that is not possible. She might have an accident on the carpet and that would be difficult to clean." The clerk spoke officiously. "This floor is easy to clean but not the carpeted areas."

I wondered how I could get the dog a breather from her cage as well as some safe exercise?

"Would it be possible to put a collar on her and use a leash to walk her outside the store? I'd like to see how she does on a leash and on grass."

"Uhhh, I don't know about that, *señor*."

"Perhaps you could ask your supervisor? You could go with me to make sure the dog is returned if you're concerned about dognapping. Would you please ask?"

"Uh . . . I don't know," the clerk said.

"Please ask? Your supervisor will either say no or yes."

"Well . . . okay. I'll call."

Thank goodness!

The clerk was gone about five minutes. I held my breath as the door from the back room opened and he reemerged. He had a smile on his face.

"My supervisor said the dog may be taken outside, but I have to stay here. However, you will be accompanied by one of our security guards. He'll be here in a few minutes with a pass that you'll need to show the guard at the store's entrance. It will let him know you have permission to take the dog out of the building."

"Wonderful," I said, picking up the puppy and

holding her to my chest while tolerating a few licks.

I scratched her head while the clerk selected a red collar that matched the pup's neck size. Next, a leash was chosen and clipped onto the collar. She pawed at the collar for a second then stopped. Next, she turned her attention to my index finger, which she playfully chewed.

"There," the clerk said, "that collar and leash should work."

The puppy stopped chewing my finger and started licking my neck and face. I Chuckled at her antics.

A security guard entered the department.

"I'm Juan," the guard said, extending his hand to the clerk.

The clerk shook his hand and said, "This is *Señor* Frank. He will be taking this puppy for a walk outside."

I shook the guard's hand. "*Mucho gusto,*" I said. "Nice to meet you. Do you have the pass we need to take the puppy out of the store?"

"*Si señor*, I have pass," Juan said, pulling a piece of white paper from his shirt pocket.

"Well then, it appears we're ready to go for a walk. Shall we get started?"

The guard nodded and led us out of the department.

With the puppy clutched to my chest, we made our way to the escalator. Along the way, several shoppers stopped to admire the puppy and pet her head. She delighted in the attention, wagging her tail nonstop.

Having reached the first floor, we headed for the main exit. There a guard smiled and petted the pup's head.

"Bought yourself a dog?" he asked.

"No," I said, turning to my chaperone, this guard

and I are going to take the puppy for a walk around the parking lot. Juan, will you please show the guard our pass?"

My escort handed the pass to the door guard who read it, signed it and then handed it back. "Have a nice walk."

Heat and humidity levels were high, and I didn't want to walk around the parking lot under the blazing sun. We headed for the shady side of the building. The parking lot had a number of elevated areas containing grass, which separated parking areas. Each grassy area contained a number of trees that provided shade. That is where we needed to go.

The black asphalt pavement was too hot for the pup's tender feet, so I carried her until we got to one of the grassy areas.

I placed her on the grass then gave the leash a lot of slack. She sniffed the grass then locked onto an interesting odor. She pulled at the leash. Her nose followed the scent as if her life depended on tracking down its source.

Juan and I followed her lead. I let out more of the spooled leash as she sniffed her way from tree to tree.

Her search was interrupted by the flight of a yellow butterfly flitting just above the top of the recently mowed grass. At one point, I thought the puppy had snared it in her mouth only to find it had escaped by millimeters. She reared up on her back legs and clawed the air as if she was about to fly in pursuit.

No doubt, this was the first time the dog had ever seen, walked on grass, or chased a butterfly. She was having fun as was Juan who smiled each time the excited puppy began a new experience.

"Do you have a dog?" I asked.

"No, but I would like to own one sometime."

"Is there a particular breed you like?"

"I love this kind of dog. We call them hot dogs, but I could never afford one. They're expensive."

I chuckled then said, "By American standards, this dog is expensive—particularly at this store. In the States, you could buy one for about $400.00."

"Even that would be too much for me."

The puppy tugged against the leash as she explored her new world and sniffed at odors not discernible by humans. She squatted to "relieve" herself then returned to exploring the grass.

I looked at the smiling guard. "Would you like to walk her?" I asked.

"Oh, I couldn't do that."

"Why not?"

Juan was silent for a moment, squishing his face with his hand as he tried to think of an answer.

"Well, you're the one who's buying the dog not me."

I raised my hand to shield my eyes from the sun as I stared at him. "Let's say I wanted to see how she reacted to other people walking her, and I needed your assistance to make that assessment. That would be okay, wouldn't it?"

Juan's face went blank. For a moment, he was silent then smiled. "Well, I guess so. If that's what you want."

"Well then. You take the leash. Let's see how she reacts to your lead."

Juan took the leash. His face lit up like a child's on seeing their first Christmas tree.

"Wow . . . This is great!" Juan's smile almost engulfed his entire head.

The puppy attempted to move onto the hot asphalt, but *Juan* knew that would not be good for her feet, so he picked her up. She licked his fingers causing him to giggle like a third-grade girl after her first boy-kiss.

199

"Put her back on the grass," I said.

"Yeah . . . She needs to stay off the hot pavement."

Juan continued to walk the dog for a few more minutes then said, "Here, you had better take the leash."

"Don't you like walking her?"

"I do, but I'm not here to walk her. You're the one to do the walking. Besides, I don't want my boss to see me goofing off."

"You're not goofing off! You're helping me asses her."

I took the leash and let the dog continue sniffing her new world.

"Well, we've been here long enough," I said, feeling a touch of sadness. "The clerk must be wondering what has happened to his dog. Maybe we should take her back."

"Yeah, we've been here about twenty minutes," Juan said, looking at his watch.

"Would you like to carry her back to the store for me?"

"Would you mind?" Juan asked, eyes wide with excitement.

"No, not at all! Take her."

I handed the pup to *Juan* who held her against his chest. Given his loose grip, she clawed her way to his chin and licked his face.

"She's wonderful," Juan said then chuckled.

The dog and Juan were bonding. I felt sorry for both of them because I knew he could never own her.

As we reached the entrance, Juan handed me the pup. He pulled the pass from his pocket and handed it to the entrance guard.

"I hope the two of you had a good time exercising the puppy," the door guard said. "I got a glimpse of you guys walking her as I made my rounds. She seemed to have a good time chasing that butterfly."

Juan and I said, "We had a wonderful time."

The guard signed the pass, noted the time of our return, and then handed the pass to Juan.

The three of us made our way to the pet department.

We were greeted by the clerk. Looking at his watch, he said, "How did everything go?"

"The dog had a wonderful time," I reported. "She responded well to the leash. She did some pulling, but in general, she tolerated the leash and the collar quite well."

Juan extended his hand "I must go, but I hope you and the puppy have a long, happy relationship."

I shook Juan's hand. "Thanks for your help."

I placed the pup on the slick floor where she repeated her unsuccessful attempts to walk.

"She walked so much better on the grass than this slick floor," I said.

"Sorry I didn't get to see that," the clerk said.

Behind me, I heard loud laughter of an approaching female. I looked up from the puppy to see a short, rotund woman who looked to be seventy years of age. She wore a flowing, purple dress that exposed far too much cleavage. She wore a thick layer of pale face powder that extended down onto her chest. Her gray roots could be seen through her bleached-blond hair that had been tightly wound, 1920s style.

Wow! She's a little over dressed for this hour.

Chandelier earrings swung from her sagging ear lobes. The ear holes were stretched to the point of almost tearing through their thresholds. I wondered if the sparkle of the earrings came from diamonds or cubic zirconium.

Several gold-colored bracelets jingled from each wrist and rings adorned eight of her digits.

Accompanying her was a tall, skinny man who

201

could have been her great grandson. You might have thought the couple to be newlyweds from the way they held on to each other and giggled.

He sported a thin moustache and wore three gold chains over his exposed hairy chest. His black shirt, printed with large red flowers, was unbuttoned to his navel. Several rings, presumably containing diamonds, sparkled from four of his fingers.

I wondered, if he had bought his jewelry or if they where gifts from—who knows? His grand-mother?

"Oh, look," the woman said, "A baby dachshund. I *love* baby dachshunds."

The way she said "I love baby Dachshunds" was disconcerting, in that it sounded as though she enjoyed them crispy and well done.

I unhooked the leash from the puppy's collar, so she was free to move about. She slipped and slid toward the woman who picked her up. As if on cue, the puppy clawed her way to the woman's face and began to lick her chin and nose.

I held my breath for fear the puppy might ingest some of the beauty queen's makeup and die.

I wondered if I should suggest the woman not permit the puppy to lick her face—for sanitary reasons? I didn't want to tell her I was afraid her makeup might kill the puppy.

"I wouldn't let the puppy lick my face if I were you," I said. "You never know what the puppy licked last."

We knowingly smiled at each other.

"You're right," the woman said and giggled, holding the pup high over her head. "Oh, you're a wonderful little girl aren't you," she gushed, looking up at the almost airborne pup. "I have two miniature Dachshunds at home, and I've been thinking of getting another one. How would you like to come and live with us?"

The clerk said, "She's a wonderful puppy. She has had all her shots and has been checked by a veterinarian. We have all her papers." The clerk smiled then said, "*She* has a pedigree."

The woman placed the pup on the floor as her escort and the clerk huddled around.

I backed away to allow more space for the woman to assess the pup. After a minute, I backed up more. I took my gun bag from the corner then left the department and the sounds of laughter evoked by the antics of the puppy.

I made my way down the escalator then past the entrance guard to whom I had spoken to earlier.

"What? No dog?" he asked.

"Not today. I think someone else is going to buy her."

I rushed to my car to get out of the heat. I rolled down the windows, started the air conditioner, and then drove away smiling.

Maybe I should not have put so many people to so much trouble over the puppy, knowing I wasn't going to buy her, but I couldn't leave knowing she had had so little human contact, lacked exercise, and had no knowledge of the outside world.

No, my actions were nothing less than an act of Christian charity. Besides, Juan not only had a reprieve from the drudgery of his routine, he had the experience of a short period of ownership of a thoroughbred dog. His time with the puppy had put a smile on his face and brought joy to his and my heart.

Frank, I said to myself, *You did well!*

Several weeks later, I learned the gaudy woman had purchased the puppy.

Every child should have two things: a dog and a mother who lets him have one.

Anonymous

Chapter 8

Bandit

Do dogs comprehend death as do human beings?

Death comes in a variety of ways for Yucatecan dogs: old age, parasites, infected wounds, ruptured internal organs resulting from fights or car collisions, bleeding from severe bites, cancer, poisons, and bone marrow suppression secondary to tick-borne diseases. All of the above are common maladies in the feral dog population of Yucatan beach communities.

Few locals care about these problems because dogs are considered a disposable life form. They are unwanted, even feared, because they may spread disease, but worse is the fact they reproduce, leading to extra mouths that vie for scraps of food.

Halfway between the villages of Chelem and Yucalpaten is a local watering hole popular with natives and *gringos*. The front of the building is open, allowing air to flow unobstructed through the dining area. Red and white checkerboard oilcloths cover tables, many of which are adjacent to a sidewalk.

207

Imagine tables crowded with hungry diners. Before them are piles of fish, calamari, shrimp, octopus pulp, refried beans, tortilla chips, pulled pork, ceviche, and several Mayan specialties, all common fare for locals. Rarely will all this food be consumed at one sitting. Many guests will take some home. Others will throw morsels to stray dogs who gather nearby.

The restaurant owner dislikes diners feeding strays, which often creep to within a foot or two of tables, but customers feed them anyway. When the owner insists dogs not be fed tableside, determined customers will drop food in a vacant field across the road from the restaurant. This often leads to fierce dog fights.

Lazy patrons try hurling their offering across the two-lane road, into the vacant field. All too often, the pitcher has a weak arm, or poor aim, and the food lands between the field and the restaurant.

When food lands on the road, hungry dogs scramble for it. They can be totally unaware of passing cars. This has led to innumerable near-collisions between dogs and cars driven by sober, as well as intoxicated, drivers. Most of the time, the dogs escape with a mouthful of food, but sometimes, a stray will die from being struck by a car.

More often than not, it is the weaker animal that gets struck by a car. Many of these weak, starving dogs are already near death. Driven by intense hunger, they are often so weak they can't avoid oncoming cars.

The restaurant owner is one of the few locals who, out of concern for his business, will remove a dog carcass from the road. Decomposition on the café's doorstep doesn't entice diners or improve one's appetite.

The numbers of pack-dogs that frequent the

restaurant varies. They include the sick, dying, and too often, pregnant females.

Over a week of trial and error, I was able to get some of these pack-dogs to follow me along a sand road that runs perpendicular to the asphalt road in front of the restaurant. I accomplished this by dropping dog treats from the window of my moving car.

When the pack and I were a block from the main road, I would sit in the sand and wait until the pack approached me. I would then scatter dry food in a circle around me so each dog had a chance to get something before larger dogs pushed smaller ones away. The law of the jungle ruled. There was no chivalry here, nor did the pack give any quarter to pregnant bitches.

One of the pack-dogs was a frequent "client" of mine. I called her Blackie. She was short in stature and underweight. I presumed she had intestinal parasites, a common condition in most Yucatecan dogs. She had a long, coarse black coat—and unusual trait for dogs in this part of the country. I pitied her having to live with so much hair in Mexico's heat. There was a two-inch hairless area on her left upper shoulder that appeared to be a recent wound. In addition, she was pregnant.

At my circular feeding ritual, she was able to get a few bites of food before being intimidated and pushed away by larger, aggressive dogs. They snarled and snapped at her, causing her to flee to the safety of a nearby pile of demolition debris.

Once in her safe place, I would stroll there and feed her puppy food. It had more nutrition for her unborn puppies as compared to the food I feed the pack.

Rarely did any of the other dogs follow me; they were too busy snapping at each other to notice my departure.

Every few days, I repeated the feeding ritual.

Blackie always retreated to the debris pile where I quietly fed her. Over time, I watched her belly expand as new life grew inside. After a few weeks, she had developed enlarged teats. I knew her delivery date was near.

A couple of weeks later, I went to feed the restaurant pack-dogs. Blackie wasn't there, so I wondered if she had had her pups.

I spread dry food for the pack and walked to the debris pile where I peered into the darkness under the concrete rubble. I didn't see or hear anything.

Damn, I hope she hasn't gone to a different spot to deliver.

I pushed a handful of puppy food as far under the debris as I could, thinking the larger pack-dogs would not be able to get it, but Blackie would.

I left wondering where she had gone.

The next day, I returned to the debris pile, flashlight in hand. I discovered the puppy food was gone. I wondered if Blackie had eaten it, or had some passing stray eaten it?

Pushing glass shards aside, I crawled through the sand to different spots along the perimeter of the debris. Every few feet, I would peer inside. I hoped to see the new mother. Occasionally, I used my flashlight to get a better view of whatever might be hiding in the darkness, but Blackie was nowhere to be seen.

On the north side of the heap, I shined my flashlight into the depths of the pile and was happy to see light reflected from two shining objects—eyes.

"Blackie, are you alright?"

Her tail wagged as she extended her neck and sniffed the air.

"Hmmm." *I guess she smells my dog food.*

I tried to throw a few bits of the dry food in her direction, but they ricocheted off the debris and fell short of the target. Blackie recoiled as though she thought I had tried to hit her. She backed away, revealing several black furry mounds.

"Oh, my God, Blackie. You've had your pups."

Blackie did not like it when I used my flashlight. She looked away from the light whenever it was shined near her face.

"Okay little doggie I won't bother you anymore."

I placed a handful of dog food deep under the debris, so the pack-dogs couldn't reach it and then left.

I returned to the debris pile a day later, with food and a water bowl for the new mother. I always kept a water-filled milk jug in my car and used it to fill various water bowls I had scattered about the community.

I got down on my hands and knees then turned on my flashlight. I discovered the food, left the day before, was gone.

"Blackie, I hope you're the one who ate the goodies."

After a few seconds of searching under the pile, I spotted Blackie.

"Hello, girl. How're you doing?"

Blackie sniffed the air and wagged her tail. Unfortunately, I could not see her pups.

Oh well. Maybe I'll see the pups tomorrow.

I left dry food and pushed the empty watering bowl farther under the debris then chuckled at my stupidity.

Frank, how are you going to fill a water bowl you can't reach?

I removed the bowl then filled it to the brim. Trying not to spill any of the water, I maneuvered the bowl to its resting spot with ninety percent of the water inside.

Blackie sniffed the air, and much to my surprise, she crept toward the bowl. She drank as though she had not had a drink in days. Having had her fill, she turned and crawled back to her pups.

She must have had more thirst than hungry if she ignored the food.

Before Blackie reached her nursery, I pointed the flashlight's beam toward the puppies. I saw three pups and all were as black as their mother.

I can't wait to get a closer look at you guys.

I returned to the debris pile on a daily basis to feed the new mother. I planned my arrival to coincide with the time the restaurant would be filled with diners. At lunch time, the dog-pack would huddle nearby, waiting for food scraps. This allowed me to feed Blackie without interference from the pack.

Some days, the restaurant owner was happy to give me food scraps, which I used to entice the dogs away from his restaurant. This was a win–win situation for the pack, Blackie, and the owner.

On a few visits to the debris pile, I would hear a puppy's whine, but most of the time the puppies slept, so I left food and water then drove away.

Somewhere between the fourth and fifth week after their birth, I saw the pups staggering about, but they stayed close their mother. I never saw them venture from their home of concrete shards.

One of these days, you'll come out, and I'll get a better look at you guys.

Time passed and the pups grew. It was about week seven, when I arrived for my daily appraisal of their situation, that I saw one pup walking a foot from the rubble. As I approached it, the puppy scampered to the safety of the debris.

A second or two later, Blackie waddled into the sunlight and stared at me as if to ask, 'Who are you and what are you doing to my pup?'

"It's just me, Blackie," I said, "I'm not going to hurt your puppies. Don't worry."

Blackie sniffed the air, wagged her tail and laid in the shade of a concrete shard that protruded from the heap like a cantilevered roof.

I was cautious not to get too close. I didn't want to frighten her or have her think I meant harm to her puppies.

I dropped a handful of dry food under the heap, filled her water bowl, and then retreated to the comfort of my air-conditioned car. I watched her waddle to the food and eat.

"See you tomorrow," I said, driving away.

That evening, I phoned my vet.

"What can I do for you, Frank?" he asked.

"I've been caring for a feral dog and her pups, for eight weeks. I think it's time to find them a forever home. How do you feel about playing dog catcher?"

"How about Monday?"

"Sounds good to me."

"Where are they?"

"They're under a pile of broken concrete one block behind the Blue Seafood Restaurant. Can we meet there at one o'clock?"

"See ya then. Oh, by the way, is the mother with them?"

"Yes, and she's doing well."

"Good. We'll want to bring her in too. I'll treat her if she needs it. We'll let her nurse the pups for another week or so to pass on more of her immunity while waiting for someone to adopt them."

"You had better bring a snare."

"Okay, see you Monday."

Monday morning, I waited in my car near the

debris pile.

In a short time, the vet arrived. He parked in the shade of a broad *Tulipan* tree, covered with large pink

blossoms, and lowered his windows.

"*Buenos tardes*," he said, exiting his car. "Where are the pups?"

"Come, I'll show you."

It was a hot day, causing us to sweat as soon as we left our cars.

We walked through broken glass and marble-sized pieces of broken concrete. At the edge of the rubble pile, we cleared away glass shards and other debris then got down on our hands and knees to peer into the darkness under the pile. Using my flashlight, we spotted the pups.

Blackie wasn't with them. The larger of the pups sniffed the air and crept toward my outstretched hand, which held a puppy sized treat. With its nose extended just beyond the edge of the concrete slabs, it took the treat and raised its head allowing me to pet it.

"Bet this is the first time you've had your head scratched," I said.

I moved my scratching hand further along the back of the puppy as it moved a few steps forward.

"Grab it" the vet said.

I gripped the pup's back and belly and extracted it from under the rubble. The pressure of my grip forced air from its stomach, producing a loud belch. This melded with the whines of discontent to produce a sour note as the puppy struggled to get free.

"Let me have him," the vet said. 'I'll take him to the car. I have a box waiting for him."

The vet took the pup to the car as I continued to monitor the other pups under the debris.

"Come out, pups," I called. "Come to papa."

The second and third pup approached us, and

when close enough, we captured them. They were also placed in the box in the vet's car.

I had been wrong about the number of puppies and their having black coats. A previously unseen pup had a white coat except for black circles around each eye. It cowered under the heap.

"Look," I said, focusing my flashlight on the puppy's face. "That one looks a like a raccoon. You know—a masked bandit kind of face. We should call that one Bandit."

"Sounds like an appropriate name," the vet said, "but don't you think we should let the new owners choose the name?"

"Okay, but first, we have to catch it; *then* they can name it."

We called and cajoled the remaining puppy for about fifteen minutes. The vet and I sweated profusely as we sat in the sand, waiting for the puppy to make its exit.

Finally, the reluctant pup reached the perimeter of the debris, extended its nose, and sniffed the air. Having sized up the situation and finding it non-threatening, the pup cautiously walked from under the pile.

"Grab it!" the vet yelled.

The pup instantly ran back under the debris.

"Damn it, Doc! You frightened him."

"Calm down," the vet said. "He'll come out. Be patient."

"I don't know how long I can sit in the sun and be patient. I don't do heat very well."

"Then sit in your car. Start your air conditioning. I'll wait here for the pup."

I retreated to my car and started the air conditioner. *God, what a relief.* From the comfort of the cool interior, I watched the vet crawl about in the sand. I saw him mouthing words, but I was unable to read his lips. I would later learn that much of what he said was unfit for polite company.

Fifteen minutes later, the vet came to my car. His head low, he looked like a defeated man.

I lowered my window. Hot, humid air carried the sweating vet's lamentations into the car.

"Damned if I know what to do," he said. "Several times it moved toward me, then, for one reason or another, it went deeper under the pile. Let's get a beer. I need to cool off. We can come back in a little while and have another go at it."

"What about the pups in your car?"

"They'll be no worse off in the shaded car than they were under the rubble. All the windows are open. Don't worry; they won't overheat during the time we cool off.

Ceiling fans buzzed overhead at the open-air restaurant, but they did little to reduce the misery of the oppressive humidity. We drank a couple of frosty beers, enjoyed some snacks, and discussed ways to capture the remaining pup.

After the beers and a lengthy discussion, we decided to try the vet's long-handled snare. If we were lucky, we might be able to get the rope around the puppy's neck and pull him from the rubble. If not, we didn't know what to do short of waiting at the pile until the puppy's need for food and water forced him out. That, however, was not something to which I looked forward.

We went back to the concrete heap.

The vet removed the snare from his trunk and connected its three sections, making it a twelve-foot long retrieving pole. A loop of rope dangled from the end opposite the grip.

I, with my flashlight, and the vet, with his snare,

crawled around the heap, trying to spot either Blackie or Bandit. We saw the pup, but Blackie was God knows where.

"See the pup?" the vet asked. "Keep your light on it, and I'll see if I can get the snare near enough to capture him."

"Okay, Doc, but keep your arm out of the light, or we won't see anything." I chuckled, "Light doesn't pass through shoulders."

"Sorry," he said, moving the pole deep into the depths of the heap. In a strained voice, he muttered, "The end of the pole is near the pup, but . . . I can't get the loop opened."

"How about pulling the pole out. I'll wedge a dog treat onto to the end of it. If you're careful, you might be able to get the food to one of those clearings then snag the loop on a piece of concrete. If we're lucky, the loop will open. If you can do that, maybe you can manipulate the pole and the loop, so it encircles the treat on the ground. Then all you have to do is wait for the puppy to investigate. When he steps inside . . . close the loop."

"You make it sound so easy," the vet said, a tinge of sharpness to his voice.

"How would you like to do this?"

"Absolutely not. I'm not very dexterous. You do it."

The vet tried several times to open the loop, but each time, he failed, and the pup moved deeper into the darkness.

"Damn it," the vet exclaimed.

"Relax. Take a deep breath. Don't give up."

"Oh, shush. Can't you see I'm working?"

"Sorry, *Doctor*."

The vet repeatedly pulled and pushed the pole, attempting to open the snare while muttering, "Damn it. Damn it."

He sweated even more, causing sand to stick to his arms and legs. Two flies persistently attempted to dine on his sweaty legs. I intervened by swatting at them.

I removed my hat, wiped my brow, and tossed the hat to the sand. The hat made me sweat more than if I didn't wear it.

The vet murmur something.

"What?" I asked.

"Thank god. I got the loop opened. Now all we have to do is wait."

"Not long I hope. I'm starting to sweat and you know I don't like to sweat."

"You can always wait in the car," the vet said, gruffly.

We sat motionless on the sand for a few minutes then the vet scanned the heap's interior with the aid of my flashlight. I, on the other hand, wiped sweat every three seconds.

"Shush," the vet whispered, "The puppy seems to be moving toward the treat. Come on little puppy . . . come on."

"Look. Here comes Blackie," I said, watching her approach us from the rear. "What should we do?"

"Sit still and offer her a treat. See if you can get her to come to you. If she does, grab her."

I made some clicking sounds, extended my hand, and wiggled a treat to get her attention.

She sniffed the air then warily approached the food. Slowly, I retracted my hand, hoping she would come close enough for me to grab her.

"Come on Blackie . . . come on," I whispered.

She inched closer and closer. Finally, she extended her head to get the treat. As she mouthed it, I grabbed her by the neck. She dropped the treat, yelped, and wiggled fiercely.

I was afraid she might break her neck, if she continued to squirm. With both hands, I drew her close to my chest and tried to calm her with quiet words and gentle back strokes. In a minute or so, she calmed down but continued to try to escape my clutch.

"Should I put her in the car with the pups?" I asked.

"*Si*, in the box, but I doubt she'll stay there . . . but who knows? She may stay with her pups, or she may try to get out of the car."

The vet looked at me. "Make sure you check yourself for fleas and ticks later."

I cuddled Blackie to my chest and took her to the vet's car. Her normal body heat plus the solar effect on her black coat made her feel like a hot coal against my chest. She also had a doggie odor I didn't like.

Damn. We both need a bath.

The puppies were whining, probably due to fright and hunger. I placed Blackie in the puppies' box and waited to see how she would react. She sniffed each pup then lay down to let them nurse.

Thank God she didn't try to get away.

"How are you doing?" I asked the vet.

"The damn puppy isn't moving. I don't know what to do. We can't take the mother and leave the puppies. Damn it. We should have her, so the other puppies can nurse."

"Well, Doc, while you're thinking about it, I'm going to spend some time in your air-conditioned car."

"Think I'll join you. I don't know what else to do except wait and see if the last pup comes out, looking for . . . whatever."

The vet and I sat in the car for a short time. The boxed puppies were quiet, and Blackie appeared to be asleep.

The vet and I discussed our options and decided the three captured pups would survive at the hospital without Blackie, but the last pup should not be left alone to fend for itself. Blackie had to be returned to the wild for the sake of her remaining puppy.

Reluctantly, I woke Blackie then carried her to the edge of the rubble. She sniffed the ground, ate the few treats we had left behind then disappeared into the depths of the debris.

"I guess she's feeding the last pup," I called to the vet.

"Guess so. Come back tomorrow and leave more food and water. Who knows, you might find the pup running around, and you can catch it. Catching mom again shouldn't be too difficult."

Feeling frustrated, we left without looking back.

Several weeks had passed, and the vet found homes for the three puppies.

I made frequent visits to the pack at the restaurant and the rubbish pile. Every once in a while, I saw and fed Blackie. She seemed to be doing well. Occasionally, I saw Bandit and discovered *it* was a male. His reaction to humans suggested he feared them. Perhaps because of the ordeal the vet and I had put him through.

About the time Bandit would have been six months old, I didn't see him anymore. I inquired of the restaurant employees if they had seen him. Their answer was always "*NO*, and "we're glad he's not around."

I was saddened by Bandit's absence. I convinced myself that, because he was so cute, someone had adopted him, or worse—he was dead from one of the grim reapers that stalked the neighborhood.

Life in the beach community went on in its slow,

inimitable way.

I managed to catch Blackie, had her spayed, and made periodic food runs to the area behind the restaurant frequented by pack-dogs whose numbers waxed and waned.

I often ate at the restaurant because the food was good. Their beer was cheap and the free snacks were tasty. However, I soon forgot about Bandit. He became old history.

During Easter Holy Week celebrations, called *Semanta Santa*, beach communities are crowded. Beach houses are opened for parties and family gatherings made possible by the temporary closing of schools and many work sites.

Highway traffic at the beach during this time is heavy and often moves no faster than five miles an hour. Car occupants wave and shout to old friends not seen in months. Some drivers stop in the middle of the road, get out of their car, and hug the driver of another car. No one is in a hurry.

Grocery stores and ice houses do a booming business as staples and party goods disappear from shelves into shopping bags and then to luxury cars or sputtering wrecks.

Many *gringos* living in Yucatan are surprised to learn that turkeys, native to Mexico, are raised on the east side of Merida, the capital of Yucatan. There are as many turkeys eaten during Mexico's observance of Easter week as are eaten at Thanksgiving in the United States.

Many locals discard turkey bones inappropriately. Invariably, stray dogs eat the bones, which easily splinter. The shards can get caught in dogs' throats, causing perforations or obstruction of the dog's esophagus. Such occurrences are often

221

associated with bleeding, infections or starvation due to the dog's inability to swallow.

Late Easter eve, I drove past the popular seafood restaurant behind which I often fed stray dogs. There wasn't much traffic at the time, so I was able to drive thirty miles an hour. I watched the passing scenes of family gatherings, barbecues, drinking parties, and children playing simple games in sandy front yards.

Suddenly, I saw something streak from the left shoulder of the road and head toward my car. "Oh my God," I said, slamming on my brakes. The rear of my car leapt into the air, secondary to my sudden deceleration and inertia. "What the hell was that?"

The tires of the car behind me screeched. The suddenly stopped car "tapped" my rear bumper. I looked in my rearview mirror to see the driver slap his forehead.

I shook my head. *God, I Hope he's alright.*

I and the other driver pulled halfway off the road and got out of our cars to inspect our damages. Fortunately, there were none. The other driver got in his car then left.

As I prepared to leave, I looked to the right side of the road and saw a white dog rummaging through a plastic shopping bag on the porch of a house where there didn't appear to be anyone home. Only the back half of the dog's body extended from the bag.

That lucky dog has found some garbage to eat.

Yucatecans use plastic shopping bags as garbage bags, which are taken to dumps. It is not uncommon to see dogs pilfering food scraps from these bags.

A passing car blew its horn. In response to the horn, the rummaging dog pulled it head from the bag.

"Oh, my God. That's Bandit."

I got a box of dog treats from my glove box and took a handful to offer Bandit a meal. With his head inside the bag, he was oblivious to my approach. I could see he was interested in what looked like a discarded, uncooked turkey. Its ankle end stuck out of the bag.

In Yucatan, it is not uncommon for food to spoil because many homes have no refrigerators or experience power failures that last three days. Other households, using ice boxes, can lose food because their ice melted, or the owner waited too long to order ice, or stores are sold out.

I dropped a treat, thinking Bandit would prefer my food to the spoiled turkey leg. He didn't. I made some clicking sounds and dropped another treat, hoping to attract his attention. He looked at me for a second then went back to gnawing the turkey inside the bag. I could see he had bitten off a chunk and was going for more.

As I prepared to drop another treat, an elderly woman startled me as she exited the house. I could tell by the way she dressed she was not wealthy.

She took one look at the dog on her porch and screamed, "Oh no! Get away! Get!" She flailed her arms as if trying to levitate and ran toward the dog yelling, "Shoo! Get!"

Unable to free the turkey leg from the shopping bag, the dog ran, clenching the leg in his teeth. This resulted in his dragging the trash bag over the sandy front yard then through a water puddle.

"Drop it. Drop it!" the woman yelled. "Drop it!"
She's afraid he'll eat bone shard, I thought.

Fearing Bandit might eat the bones and injure himself, I chased him. I managed to step on the bag, thinking I could stop the theft of the garbage and spoiled turkey leg. However, between the forward motion of the dog, its hold on the turkey leg, and my pinning the bag to the sand, the bag tore open and the dog ran off with a whole turkey.

The woman and I stood side-by-side, watching the dog and the turkey carcass disappear behind an abandoned house two hundred feet down the road.

With worry on her face and despair in her voice, the woman dropped her arms. "That was my Easter dinner."

"Oh, God. I'm so sorry. I thought the dog had found a garbage bag with a *spoiled* turkey. I had no idea there was a fresh turkey inside."

"I left the groceries for a minute while I stored my other groceries. I meant to come right back, but my husband called me to the backyard." She shook her head and sighed. "I took too long to get back. Pedro is going to kill me."

I empathized with the poor woman. Money and food are in short supply for the average citizen here.

"Would you allow me to help?" I asked.

"What can you do?" she asked. "The turkey is ruined."

"I'd like to help you get another turkey. Will you accept this 200-peso bill?"

The woman's face broadened as her lips pushed wrinkled cheeks backward into the happiest smile I had seen in years. Her eyes twinkled then a tear ran down her cheek. She took the bill then clasp my hand between hers. "May the Holy Virgin bless you and your family."

"You're most welcome. I hope you have a happy Easter."

As I drove away, I saw the woman waving at a local bus headed for Progreso. She was, no doubt, on her way to buy another turkey. I hoped she would be more careful with the second one.

A year earlier, I had named a dog Bandit because of his mask-like face. Little did I know he would grow up to become a real bandit.

I never saw Bandit again.

Chapter 9

Scooter

Damn, it's hot today, I said to myself.

As if from a furnace, a blast of hot air greeted me as I opened my car door. I had been in the grocery store ten minutes. How could the car have gotten so hot so quickly? I started the air conditioner and noted the car's thermometer registered the out-side temperature at 101°F.

Sweating, I drove toward the road leading out of Progreso and passed another grocery store. The new store stood on what had been a parking lot for eighteen-wheeler trucks. The empty lot had been home to numerous stray dogs that used the bushes at the lot's western border as a refuge. In the past, I often stopped there to drop food and leave water for the dogs who roamed the area, looking for a truck driver who would give them a few scraps of a sandwich or taco.

As I passed the driveway between the new store and the old row of bushes, I saw four adult dogs lying in the shade of the bushes, panting.

Given this heat, guess I should give them some water.

I pulled onto the edge of the driveway then parked. Two of the dogs approached my car, tails wagging. No doubt, they wanted food and needed water. I went to my trunk and got a jug of water then scanned the area for something to use as a water bowl.

Lying just under the north end of the bushes, I saw a baby's faded-pink plastic bathing tub. I pulled it free of entangling vines and examined it. It had a hole in the bottom of the deep end.

This will work if I keep the water in the shallow end.

I dropped the tub in the shade of the bushes, close to the pack. At first, they scattered, but soon, it was all I could do to pour water without spilling it as the dogs pushed their way to the tub and lapped at the liquid.

"For God's sake, calm down."

After the tub had been emptied, I made small piles of dog treats several feet apart, parallel to the bushes. Each dog would have something to eat without having to fight for food.

A brief episode of growling and bearing of fangs occurred between two of the larger dogs at the first pile. However, the dogs soon realized there were several piles of food and separated to conquer their own. It didn't take long for each pile to be eaten, and then the dogs looked at me as if to ask, 'Is there more?'

I debated about giving them more food, but I decided to save what food I had. I wanted to feed other dogs I knew I would encounter farther down the road.

I started to return to my car when something to my right caught my eye. Something, low to the pavement, awkwardly crept toward me.

"Oh, my God. It's a puppy."

I guessed the puppy to be about twenty-weeks

old. It scooted and dragged itself forward using only its front paws. It moved in a zig zag fashion, pulling itself first with the right paw then the left. Splayed against the asphalt, its rear legs lay flat. Its back feet pointed rearward and parallel to its tail. The rear legs were being dragged with no indication they were functional.

Are its legs paralyzed . . . broken?

It dawned on me the pup might be thirsty and hungry. It must have smelled the treats I gave the pack dogs and came to investigate. Sadly, it was dragging its tender underside across the scalding hot black asphalt. *Ouch!*

I walked toward the puppy but stopped a few feet away for fear of alarming it. The pup continued to crawl toward me.

Hmm. Guess he's not afraid of me.

When it was two feet away, I looked down into two sad brown eyes. They seemed fearful and pleading at the same time.

I was overcome with pity and sadness. I swallowed hard, trying to overcome my emotional reaction on seeing the pup's distress.

The pup's reddish, short coat looked clean except for its hindquarters. The rear legs and tail looked wet, probably from urine, and was covered with its own poop.

Poor thing can't stand to pee or poop.

I hurried to my trunk, got an old towel, and then returned to the pup. I used the towel to pick it up, noting it was a *he*. He whined for a few seconds.

His rear legs dangled like string. His abdomen revealed ten or twelve pustules as well as a few on the underside of his rear legs. The elbow areas of his front legs were scraped raw.

Seeing all the trauma, I said, "Oh God! I hope I didn't hurt you by picking you up."

I took him to my opened trunk and placed him inside on the towel. I did this for three reasons. I could feed him there without the other dogs stealing his food. Secondly, I wanted to get him out of the sun, and the last reason—get his belly off the hot pavement.

I broke some treats into sizes that would fit his small mouth. He attacked them in a ravenous fashion.

God, he's starved.

I needed the plastic tub, so I could give him water, but I worried if I left, the pack-dogs might jump in the trunk and eat his food or injury him. After considering several options, I lowered the trunk lid, allowing a crack of light inside.

I picked up the plastic tub then took it to the trunk, poured in a couple of ounces of water, and then tilted the tub edge under the puppy's snout. He lapped at the water with an urgency not seen from the pack-dogs. He drank it all.

Damn, you're thirsty.

No sooner than he had emptied the tub and curled his tongue in a yawn, he fell asleep. He dropped onto "all fours" so fast, I thought he had died.

"Don't die on me, puppy."

Finally, his chest moved as he took a breath.

"Thank God."

I looked at the pack-dogs I had just fed to see if one of them had teats to suggest it might have given birth to this puppy. There was no such mama dog.

Hmm. Wonder if there are there other pups. I'd better look in the bushes.

I walked the hundred-twenty-foot length of the row of bushes, scanning the ground under each low limb. I wanted to see if there were other pups, perhaps hiding or with a mother dog. I pushed all kinds of trash aside but saw no pups.

How the hell did he get here?

Returning to the trunk, I looked at the sleeping pup. "Well now, what am I going to do with you, little guy?"

It's Sunday and the vet is closed. This is not an emergency . . . so . . . better take you home and give you a bath.

I took the puppy and his towel to the passenger seat in the now cooled interior. Despite being moved, he remained asleep.

"You must be exhausted."

I phoned home and asked the caretaker to get out the old bathing tub I had used for other feral puppies.

The pup remained asleep throughout the eight-mile trip home.

As I pulled into my carport, my rescue dogs ran to the car, tails wagging and barking. My dogs' barking had awakened the pup.

I went to the passenger side of the car to get him. He stretched his front legs and looked around. There was the possibility my dog's barking had frightened him. He shivered as I picked him up, but he did not whine.

The caretaker, Juan, greeted me, holding the bathing tub I had used in the past to bathe other puppies.

"Where do you want this?" Juan asked, staring at the pup. "This one doesn't look too good. Did some-one run him over?"

"I'm not sure, but would you take the tub to the outdoor faucet then get the anti-flea soap?"

Juan walked toward the faucet. Looking over his shoulder, he said, "That one's a cripple for sure. Legs dangle too much."

Carrying the pup, I followed Juan and asked him to put the tub on the patio floor. "Would you put a couple of cups of water in the tub? I want to see if he wants a drink before I bathe him."

Water in place, I offered the pup another drink. He sniffed the water for a moment, lapped at it for a second, and then turned away.

"Guess he isn't very thirst," I said, looking up at Juan. "Put a few drops of that flea soap in the tub and then fill it half-way."

While Juan filled the tub with tepid water, I examined the pup's abdomen again, noting the pustules, numerous scrapes, and what looked like first-degree burns on his belly and the thin skin of his penis sheath. I worried that a few blisters of a second degree burn might be forming there.

These burns must be from crawling over that hot asphalt.

While the pup rested in my palm, I moved him up and down noting his heft. No question about it, he was under weight for a pup of his presumed age.

Wonder when he last saw his mother or had milk? Did she abandon him because he was injured?

Juan created lots of suds on the surface of the bath water then I lowered the pup into the warm bath, alert to the fact the water might be too warm for his burned belly.

At first, he attempted to swim with his front legs but then relaxed as I rubbed suds into his short-haired coat. Soon, the puppy had company in his swim. About twenty fleas joined the swimming competition they were destined to lose.

The dried stool and dirt, stuck to his coat, dissolved and fell from his legs and tail. In minutes, the bath was over and the pup ready to be dried.

Juan brought a towel and held it out, so I could place the pup in its middle.

Contrary to most dogs, who would be expected to shake themselves dry, this pup either did not know the ritual or wasn't able to do it. He collapsed in my palm.

Maybe he thinks I'm just being kind by rubbing his back —not drying him.

"Juan, hold him, will you. I want to get some antibiotic ointment for his scratches. Can't have him getting an infection on his belly."

I applied the ointment and bandaged his abdomen with some gauze pads and strips of gauze from my first aid kit.

Juan chuckled. "No use putting bandages on the scrapes if he is going to continue to drag them through God knows what."

I had no sooner placed the pup on the patio than Juan said, "You know he's going to pee and poop and get it all over his self—and that bandage. You have wasted your time, water, and soap."

"Well . . . I had to do it . . . to get rid of the fleas."

Juan had made a good point.

"Okay, Juan. What can we do to keep him clean?"

"We need to lift his rear off the ground."

"Hell, Juan. I know that. Do you have any suggestions?"

"Yeah, I'll get one of my grandson's logs from his building block set. We could put it under his belly near the rear legs. Maybe it will keep his 'equipment' off the ground."

"Good idea. Let's give it a try."

"Yeah, let's hope it works. I don't wanna clean up a lot of poop just because he can't get to the sand in the front yard."

Juan placed the ten-inch-long "log" under the pup's pelvis. This held his hind quarter off the ground but not far enough. His rear paws still dragged the patio as he pulled and scooted himself forward. Unfortunately, the log did not roll. It had to be dragged as the pup scooted forward.

231

"Well, that will have to do for now," I said. "We have to find something else. The log adds to his burden. I'll take him to the vet's in the morning and see what he has to say."

My rescued dogs, jealous of my attention to the pup, tried to push their heads under my hand for a scratch. They had to be pushed aside while I cared for the new arrival. With the pup being a tad more mobile than earlier, the adult dogs looked at him with puzzlement. Each time they nosed the pup, his eyes widened, and he shivered with fear.

"The dogs are making him nervous," I said looking to Juan for confirmation.

"Yeah," Juan said, nodding. "Better give him a safe space for the night or they might eat him."

"Oh God, don't say that."

"Well, he's not much bigger than the rats they eat."

"Let's clear a spot in the storage room," I said, shaking my head and watching the pup trying to move toward me. "Put down several pages of the *Dario* to keep the floor clean." I chuckled, "It'll give him something to read until tomorrow."

"Okay, but you know, you'll have to wash him again in the morning."

In my heart, I knew Juan was right. I watched as he spread the newspaper on the storage room floor.

Do I take the roller away or leave it for the night. Will it help keep him clean . . . Will he be able to sleep with it under his belly?

It dawned on me the pup had no sense of pain in his rear quarter. He wouldn't feel pain or discomfort with the log in place.

Would its pressure interfere with blood flow to the belly skin? Could its pressure cause a skin ulcer overnight?

With those thoughts running through my mind, I

232

decided I shouldn't risk adding misery to insult, so I removed the log.

"Puppy, guess you'll get another bath in the morning," I said, pushing his water and food bowls nearer his snout. Closing the door to the storage room, I left, hoping he would have a good night.

I had a restless night. Several times, I thought I heard the pup whining, but on closer listening, I decided the wind caused the noise.

The next morning, I went to the storage room and found he had pooped and peed on the paper where I had originally left him. He obviously knew he had "answered the call of nature" and had moved to a clean spot to rest and sleep.

He looked up at me with big, sad eyes and yawned. I could have sworn he smiled. He crawled toward me whining. As I rubbed his head, he pushed his head into each caress.

"Just as I expected, puppy, you need another bath."

I pushed his food and water bowl closer to his nose then went to get the tub for his bath.

Juan must have heard me moving about because he walked out of his casita. "You gonna give him a bath?"

"How'd you guess?"

"Better wait 'til after he's had his breakfast. There'll be another mess after he eats."

"You're right," I said, "but I can't stand to see him covered in all that . . . stuff."

"Well, get used to it," Juan said, shaking his head.

I removed the gauze dressing then gave the pup a quick bath and waited for the next mess to happen. I waited because I wanted to take him to the vet without him making a mess in the car or on the vet's exam table.

When the morning mess happened where expected, I felt relieved. I could now take the pup to the vet's office without worrying about having to have my car professionally cleaned.

The towel I had used to get the pup home had been thrown away, so I had to get another I could sacrifice. Having it at the ready, I picked up the pup and placed both on the passenger seat. We then headed for the vet's office.

Along the way, the occasional bump seemed to disturb the pup. He shivered. Once or twice, he whined, so I rubbed his head. That quieted him.

"Would you feel better if you were in my lap?"

I pulled to the side of the road then picked up the pup and towel and placed both in my lap. His head pointed toward my belly. I then continued the drive.

"You look like you feel better there." I said, looking down at the now sleeping pup.

I parked in front of the vet's office, wrapped the towel around the sleeping pup, and then picked him up. He stirred then yawned. I held him in front of me to admire his cuteness, and much to my surprise, he licked my nose.

Despite his handicap, he brought me a deep sense of happiness.

"My, my," the vet said on seeing the pup.

"*What* happened to him?"

"I'm not sure, but he's paralyzed in his hind quarters. I don't know if it is due to trauma or a birth defect."

"Best way to know is to X-ray him, but you know there isn't a veterinarian X-ray machine in Progreso."

The vet felt the pup's spine and hip joints then said, "Hmmm. I feel some abnormal movement. I'd

guess he was run over by a bicycle or someone stepped on his back side. If he had been run over by a car,
he would have been crushed . . . dead."

"Any chance he'll recover?"

The vet crunched his lips and appeared to be in
deep thought. "I doubt it. I think his spine and / or leg
nerves have been permanently damaged."

"And they won't heal?"

The vet frowned. "I don't think he will ever walk
on those legs."

"What should I do?"

Narrowing his gaze, the vet looked me in the eye.
"I'd suggest putting him down. He can't survive on
his own."

"I was afraid you were going to say that, but isn't
there something we can do?"

The vet walked to his desk at the back of the
room. "Let's look in here," he said, picking up a
catalog. "This company is in Mexico City. Their stuff
is expensive, but they'll have something you could
use."

We thumbed through the catalog and found a
number of ambulation assistive devices for dogs.
There were several that would no doubt add to the
pup's ability to get around, but they were expensive.
The vet made a point of telling me that the appliance
would have to be replaced several times as the pup
grew.

"That could cost a lot of money," I said.

"Give me some time to inquire around. Maybe I
can find someone to help."

"Great. Thanks. I'll come back tomorrow."

"There's an awning guy, Carlos, around the
corner," the vet said. "He works with lightweight
tubing. Maybe he can make something for you. He
also uses straps similar to those on the appliances in

the catalog, except wider. I bet he can improvise something. Talk to him . . . see what he can do."

"Good Idea. May I leave the pup here while I visit the shop? I don't want to leave him in a hot car."

"Sure."

"One more thing. May I borrow the catalog? I want to show the awning man what I want."

"Okay," the vet said, handing me the catalog. "Make sure you bring it back."

I introduced myself to Carlos.

"*Mucho gusto*" Carlos said, shaking my hand. "What may I do for you?"

I informed Carlos about Scooter, his need, and then showed him the catalog.

He stared at several of the items on page 278 then put his finger on the picture of a cart in the middle of the page. "If you get the wheels, I'll make the rest of the device. Better yet, I'll make it, so it can be expand-ed to match his growth."

"Great, but do you know where I can get the wheels—here in Progreso."

There's a bicycle shop on *Calle* 78. They do repairs and sell kid's trainer wheels. I think we could use that kind of wheel."

"Good. I'll see if I can buy some. Would you be able to start work today?"

"Not today. I have another job that's gotta be fin-ished in four hours."

"Okay. Tomorrow is good."

I visited Carlo's workspace three days later to check on the progress of the cart.

The shop owner smiled and his eyes lit up as he held up the finished cart.

"What do you think of this?" Carlos asked.

"Wow. It looks like a cart from that expensive

catalog."

I gave the wheels a spin then noted the slip joints Carlos had made, so the length of the cart could be elongated as the pup grew. "Nice. Real nice."

Carlos drew my attention to the canvas strap toward the rear of the cart. It was strung between the two tubular arms of the cart that would extend along each side of the pup's flank. The strap would hold his tail up and away from his anus, allowing him to defecate without soiling himself or the strap.

"What do I do if he soils the strap?" I asked. "It's fixed. I can't remove it as it is now. Could you redo it, so it has snaps that would allow it to be removed, cleaned or replaced if necessary?"

"No problem. I can modify it now, if you want to wait."

"Please. I don't mind waiting."

Within minutes, Carlos had added a snap to the rear of each arm of the cart and to the canvas strap.

"What do you think of that?" he asked, holding up the strap.

"Great, but could you make two more straps for future use? Maybe make some that are a little longer than this one . . . to use when he's wider."

"No problem."

While I'm thinking of it, would you make two or three more straps for holding the side bars to his flanks. We have to allow for his chest and belly to grow."

"Will do, but I'll have to start tomorrow. I don't have time today."

"Great. I'll come back tomorrow."

The next day, I brought the pup with me to the awning shop.

"Well, who do you have there?" Carlos asked, through a widening smile.

"This is Scooter. I named him that because of the way he moved when I found him.

"Okay, Scooter, let's hope you don't have to scoot anymore. Let's see how your cart fits."

I placed Scooter on a worktable and held up his rear, so we could slip the abdominal strap under his belly and then lace it up with the shoe string that would secure the strap around his torso. We then lifted his tail over the rear strap.

"Ut oh," I said. "It's too close to his anus."

We loosened the slip joint and extended the two side arms and then tightened the set screws holding the side arms in place.

"That's looking pretty good," Carlos said, lifting Scooter's tail.

"Yeah. Pretty good. Let's put him on the floor and see how he handles all this hardware.

At first, Scooter tried to bite the abdominal strap, but relented when he realized that trying to bit it was too much trouble.

I pulled a doggie treat from my pocket and fed him part of it. He liked it. I held another piece a few inches from his nose. For a second, nothing happened, but then he extended his nose toward the treat. I moved it a little farther away, and he took a half-step forward. I moved the treat a little more. He looked at it for a second then walked toward the treat.

"Wow," I exclaimed. "He's walking."

"And very well," Carlos said.

I was so happy for the puppy I didn't know what to do, so I hugged him to my chest—wheels and all. He licked my chin, and I laughed. I would like to think the lick was a "thank you" for giving him mobility.

Over the next few weeks, Scooter's front legs got stronger, allowing him to walk faster and longer while wearing the cart. Soon, he ran around, almost like a normal dog.

Sometimes, at low tide, I would take him onto the beach and let him run over the hard-packed sand. He loved it. Needless to say, the cart wheels moved easier over hard surfaces than the sand in the front yard, but he managed to get there and back after "number one or two."

I learned to give him his last food and water allowance around 11:00 p.m. This yielded an "accident free" night 95% of the time. Because of that low failure rate, I removed the cart after the last bathroom visit of the day and let him sleep in the storage room with newspapers on the floor. He didn't seem to mind.

In the mornings, the cart was laced into place at 8:00 a.m. and left until bedtime.

I shared my success story with some expat friends. The story piqued the interest of another American couple, John and Judy, who were visiting their expat friends in nearby Merida. I heard the two visitors wanted to meet Scooter, and I agreed to see them and introduce them to Scooter.

John and Judy were upbeat as they told me about the disabled dog rescue operation they ran in the United States. They asked what I had planned for Scooter.

"I'd like to find him a loving, forever home here in Mexico, if I can," I replied. "I had four rescue dogs when I brought Scooter home. Five mouths to feed and vet bills can add up, so I hope I can find him a forever home soon. Someone who would love him despite his disability.

"Maybe we can help find him a home," Judy said. "Scooter is the kind of dog that gets adopted rather quickly in the States. How would you feel about us taking him with us when we return?"

239

I was shocked. I didn't know what to say. However, reality set in, and I said, "Yes."

In a few days, we had completed the necessary paper work and Scooter, along with his extra straps, was on his way to a new home.

My heart ached a bit as he settled into Judy's arms. The farther she took him from me, the more he appeared to be anxious. I tried not to cry, but I did.

Some of the tears were for me and my loss. Some were happy tears for Scooter.

No sooner had the car driven out of sight, My heart ached a bit. I missed him.

Wow. Didn't realize I had become so attached.

I knew Scooter would fare better on grass at a home with loving "parents."

Three weeks later, Judy sent me a video of Scooter with his forever family. Wearing a flashy-red, store-bought cart, he ran around his new backyard chased by a giggling five-year-old girl.

I was so happy, I cried.

Prayer For A Dog

Dear God,

Please admit this, your creation, through
heaven's gate.
May it share in the glee of angels forever
wagging its tail with joy.
Assign an angel to pat its head and rub its
belly to its unending delight
May it never know pain, rejection, or feel
hunger and thirst.
May it know only your perpetual love as
you cuddle it in your unending, loving
embrace.
As it lives forever in my memory, grant it
eternal peace.

Amen.

Author Information

Frank Barham did his undergraduate studies at East Tennessee State University then went on to earn and M.D. degree from the University of Tennessee. After practicing medicine for a number of years, he earned a master's degree in health services administration (MSHA) and worked as a hospital administrator.

Late in life, Dr. Barham earned a master's degree in the medical humanities (MMH), from Drew University majoring, in bioethics. He continued his studies at Drew University for a doctor of letters degree (D. Lit.) in ethics.

Doctor Barham has published: *Saving the World One Dog at a Time; The Religious Right is Wrong-The Ethics of Religion; Why Republicans Are The Way They Are,* Mayan Dolls Don't Die, and *The Milk Murders.*

www.ingramcontent.com/pod-product-compliance
Lightning Source LLC
Chambersburg PA
CBHW071524040426
42452CB00008B/875